Pages of Passion Book 2

Bold Beginnings

George J Hatcher

Previously published as Billion Dollar Rainmaker Part I in 2021

This book can be purchased at over 40,000 bookstores and libraries, including brick-and-mortar stores, online, in print and digital, including Apple, Kindle, and Audible formats. Casa Hatcher Press books are available at special quantity discounts for bulk purchases, sales promotions, premiums, and educational use for fundraising. Casa Hatcher Press is a subsidiary of Pretty Face, Inc., Rancho Mirage, California 92270.

For details, contact:

Casa Hatcher Press. http://casahatcherpress.com (800) 416-6189

Copyright © 2024 by George Hatcher. All rights reserved. Printed in the United States of America and abroad.

No part of this book may be used in any manner except in the case of brief quotations in critical articles or reviews.

Book and cover designed by Casa Hatcher Press

Pages of Passion, by George J. Hatcher

First Edition 2024

LCCN: 2024947166

ISBN: 979-8-9882886-4-0 (Hardback)

ISBN: 979-8-9882886-5-7 (Paperback)

ISBN: 979-8-9882886-6-4 (Ebook - EPUB)

Reflections Unveiled: Chronicles of a Life Revisited

As you explore the rich fabric of my journey, I want to emphasize a crucial aspect of my narrative. While I've made adjustments to the names of individuals, places, and establishments for their privacy, and while memory can play tricks, one thing remains clear – the essence of this story is rooted in authenticity.

Within this collection of experiences, woven with threads of honesty and a touch of creative license, what stands firm amid flux and uncertainty is the sincerity of my encounters. So, as you navigate these pages and tread the winding paths of my life, remember this: despite the revisions and the occasional embellishment, the core of the narrative resonates with genuine emotion and truth.

Dedication

Dearest Molly,

In the dance of our journey, you are my unwavering guide,

and in every note of my life, you are the sweetest refrain.

With all my love,

George

Pictures In This Book

Dear Reader,

As you embark on this journey through my life, I want to share a unique aspect of this autobiography. Alongside my words, you will find a handful of selected images that complement my stories and memories. While these photos are not direct representations of the individuals I've written about, they serve to illustrate and evoke the essence of my experiences. For instance, my third wife is referred to as Sophia in this narrative, but it's important to note that "Sophia" is not her real name, and the AI-generated image representing her does not depict her alone; it captures the essence of a character playing the part of Sophia in my book.

In reflecting on my life, I've included images of significant people, places, and moments that shaped who I am today. From a stock photo of a child delivering canned food—reminiscent of my industrious youth when I sold canned goods I received from my father—to a vibrant portrayal of lettuce in the fields, reminding me of the days my dad took me to the lettuce fields, where workers picked lettuce and loaded his truck with crates of it, these visuals add another layer to my narrative.

Thank you for joining me on this personal journey. I hope these images enrich your reading experience and allow you to visualize my memories as vividly as I have.

WARNING!

Adult matter

This book is intended for a mature audience. It addresses themes of violence and sexual behavior that may not be suitable for minors, sensitive readers, or those navigating the complexities of our current world, marked by relentless challenges such as incurable sexually transmitted diseases and a pandemic that has forced many into isolation.

While this narrative draws from my real-life experiences, the identities of certain individuals have been modified to protect their privacy.

Please be aware that all characters, organizations, and events portrayed within these pages may have been influenced by the passage of time, selective memory, and a timeline adjusted for clarity and flow.

Works by George Hatcher

Mario Ambulance Chaser Series

Mario 1: Woman in Jeopardy

Mario 2: Coming of Age

Mario 3: Risky Business

Mario 4: Free Fall

Mario 5: Afire

Mario 6: Marked

Mario 7: Aftershock

Mario 8: Captivated

Single Titles

One Wilshire

Gabi

Rico

Cats: Meow Is The Language Of Love

HER: Artistic Expressions Through AI

Elegance In White: Through Wedding Gowns

Quinceañera Fashion: Fifteen & Fabulous

Billion Dollar Rainmaker Part I

Pages of Passion Book 1: My First 19 Years

Coming Soon

Pages of Passion Book 3: Rising Waves

Pages of Passion Book 4: Threads Of Destiny

Pages of Passion Book 5

Pages of Passion Book 6

Pages of Passion Book 7

Mario 9

Gabi 2

Rico 2

Contents

Introduction	xvii
1. Tastes Of Freedom	1
2. The Locker Thing	16
3. My New Job	28
4. The Double Life: Balancing Work, Love, and Fun	36
5. Driven by Determination and Entrepreneurial Spirit	43
6. Ensenada, Mexico	48
7. Weekend	64
8. Independence, ELA	68
9. Sophia	99
10. Lessons Unlearned	104
11. Spreading Out	112
12. Eastland Auto Center	127
13. Grand Opening	170
14. Elena	182
15. Ramirez Splits	198
16. Lunch Together a Must	214
17. No Secrets	221
18. Cash Flow Blues	235
19. Elena Kind of Moves In	240
20. I Don't Have A Jealous Bone In My Body	254
About the Author	263

Introduction

RERUN

Marriage and Disillusionment

At seventeen, I married Selena while serving in the Navy—a decision that felt thrilling at the moment. In a reckless burst of passion, I went AWOL and fled to her hometown in Mexico, where I opened an ice cream parlor in her old neighborhood, dreaming of a fresh start. But the exhilaration didn't last long; soon, my past caught up with me. The FBI tracked me down, delivering a harsh warning: they'd be back if I didn't turn myself in before I turned eighteen.

Just days before my eighteenth birthday, I discovered that Selena was having an affair with her former fiancé—the one she had sworn she was finished with. That revelation shattered our marriage.

A Desperate Escape

Introduction

One late evening, my wife's sister, Luna, drove me across the border from Mexico, with me hidden in the trunk of the car. Fear gripped me at every rumble of the tires on the pavement, especially for her safety. As we approached the crossing, I wrestled with the decision to turn myself into the Navy, which I wanted to do. I believed surrendering would be the better choice, possibly earning some leniency with the judge since I was returning on my own. However, the thought of being arrested loomed over me like a dark cloud, filling me with dread. I couldn't shake the feeling that being caught would lead to a far worse outcome than the self-surrender I was seeking.

Somehow, I made it across to El Paso and caught a train to Los Angeles. Yet, my destination for surrender was San Diego—the last place I had been stationed before going AWOL. Upon arrival, however, I hesitated, caught between fear and the desire to make things right. Instead, I found myself behind bars in a Tijuana jail, where I practically begged the shore patrol to arrest me and bring me back to the USA. The conditions in that jail were horrendous.

Facing the Consequences

I was sent to a Marine brig, serving a four-month sentence that was intense, to say the least. Even amidst the struggle, I knew I deserved it. Upon my release, I was supposed to return to the Navy to complete my four-year term, but fate had other plans. Just as I stepped out of the brig, detectives from Los Angeles arrested me on a charge of grand theft.

The allegation? Borrowing $3,500 from my girlfriend's mother under false pretenses when I was around fifteen years old. It felt surreal as the judge, in that case, sentenced me to the California

Introduction

Youth Authority and sent me to DVI, Deuel Vocational Institution—a place I insist is a prison, far from anything resembling juvenile hall. In total, I spent about 27 months incarcerated, locked away as my past decisions haunted me.

This book begins when I was released on parole. While doing time, Luna, my wife's sister, delivered my car I had left behind in El Paso.

Chapter 1
Tastes Of Freedom

I searched for a car to buy and found an old '51 Chevrolet. At noon, I met my stepdad at his work downtown, and we drove to the bank where he had deposited the money from the sale of the Ford Luna had driven from El Paso.

I offered my dad half of the money. "I owe you for the money you sent me monthly," I said. He insisted I take the whole eight hundred. He drove me to the used car lot, and I paid two hundred fifty dollars for the Chevy. Compared to my Ford, the Chevy was a rag. It had holes in the front seat and was an actual rust bucket, but it drove like a million bucks. I stopped off for a fast burger and fries just because I could, but the fries fell through the hole in the seat somewhere off-Broadway. I resolved to do something about that, then drove downtown to a department store and spent a hundred dollars on new clothes. That amount of money bought a lot of clothes then. Since I was there, and the department store seemed as good a place as any to start job-hunting, I took the elevator to Personnel and applied for a maintenance job in air-conditioning. I filled out the application and put the pharmacy down as my last place of employment.

Instead of mentioning the Navy, I wrote that I had been at the Deuel Vocational Institute (DVI), a juvenile detention center.

That was a lie. DVI was a prison. They sent juveniles there who had reached their seventeenth birthday.

I couldn't help noticing the girl at the desk.

She had shoulder-length brown hair, a fair complexion, and light-brown eyes that shimmered with something else. Her smile was so perfect it could have belonged in a toothpaste commercial. She wore a striking red dress and cherry red lipstick, a combination that would have looked inappropriate on anyone else, but on her, it was nothing short of bold.

We were alone in the office. As she looked at my application,

I could not look away from her. Suddenly, she ripped the application in half and handed me a fresh one. "You don't need to be this truthful," she said, her voice carrying a hint of a Spanish accent that I found alluring. "I don't have anything in the HVAC department, but if you need a job, I can check out what we have open while you fill this out again."

I blushed, a reaction I still remember to this day. "You can stay where you are," she said, and I found myself at her desk, across from her, filling out the second application. I watched her walk to the file cabinets behind the counter, her body moving with a captivating grace. Maybe it was the eyes of a man who had been twenty-plus months without a woman, but her body was remarkable, with a tiny waist and a bottom that could have been right out of a blue jeans commercial. But she didn't have jeans on. From what I could see of them, her legs were also beautiful. She wasn't particularly busty but was certainly adequate. In many ways, she reminded me of Selena. Her smart-looking little name badge said Alicia.

She returned to the desk.

"Gosh, George. Is it okay to call you by your name?"

I nodded. "By all means," I said.

She took out a compact, checked her face, patted it with a small pad, and dropped the make-up in the top drawer of her desk. I didn't see that the powder did anything. She applied bright red lipstick, like her dress. I didn't see that the lipstick did anything because she was already wearing it. She dropped that in her drawer, too. I think she was flirting. She smiled.

"The only thing open right now is in the custodial department."

I knew that work. In boot camp, county jail, and DVI, I had mopped more floors, cleaned more toilets, and buffed more hardwood and granite floors than I could count.

"If it's a job, I want it."

"Very cool," she said. "I'll tell you how to get to that department for an interview. If he says you're hired, come back and see me.

"Can I call you Alicia?"

"Yes, call me Alicia," she said, extending her hand across the desk.

We shook hands, and she dazzled me with that smile of hers.

She arranged an interview with Mr. Lewis on the ground floor of the custodial department. I was back in an hour. Alicia greeted me with that smile.

"Mr. Lewis just called and said he hired you. Congratulations."

She handed me a payroll card. I filled it out.

"This might seem a little awkward, but since I now have a job, would you go out with me to celebrate tonight?"

"But I don't even know you." Giggles.

"If you remove the application from the trash, that's my life story. I bought this trashy car, but it ran okay from the car lot. I have money. We don't have to do stag or anything."

Alicia was laughing away. I think she wanted to go pee. It was one of those kinds of laughs, and she was red as her dress.

"Let me recheck the application."

I leaned forward across her small desk and stared directly into her eyes. She didn't look away but toyed with the pen in her hand. She picked up the application and began to read.

"Let's see now. Your name is George Hatcher." She looked up and smiled. "Hello, George Hatcher. My name is Alicia Ponce." She turned back to the application. "Let's see. You're single?"

"Divorced," I said.

"You're young to have gone through a divorce already." She blushed a little. "I'm twenty-three, but I've never been married and don't have a steady."

"That's music to my ears," I said.

"I don't know, George. You're four years younger. You can't go clubbing till you're twenty-one." She was right, but her tone was teasing. "When did you leave that place we threw in the trash?"

"I will turn twenty in a few months, specifically in October. That's close to twenty-one. Does that work for you? (I could have shared with her my experiences of going to clubs at the age of sixteen with Christine and my early explorations of sexuality.)

"You're so young," she said like she was singing.

"Should I come back next year when I come of age?" I wasn't joking enough with the age thing.

"I'm messing with you," she said, then grew silent, staring at me and each other.

"I got released on Saturday. I promise I didn't do time for robbery, burglary, rape, or anything tremendously ugly. I was, however, guilty."

"I believe you," she said. "You must have some story to tell. Married, divorced, two years behind bars, and only nineteen years old."

"Alicia, where have you been all my life?"

She didn't reply.

I thought of standing at attention like I did in the Navy when I was in front of an officer. I didn't do that, but it sure crossed my mind.

"Where do you plan to take me?"

"Anywhere you want. Like I said, I have some money."

"After considering your application, I'd be delighted to go out with you and celebrate your new position."

I nodded.

"One condition, though," she said.

"I knew there would be a catch."

"You'll have to get me home early. You start work at three in the morning."

"Ouch," I said.

I already knew about the hours. My interviewer had told me my shift was from three to eleven in the morning.

She wrote her address on the back of her business card and gave it to me.

"Alicia, thank you. I totally scored today."

I was proud of that first day's accomplishments: a new car, new clothes, a job, and a date with Alicia Ponce.

Selena was not the only girl around. I'd known this for a long time, but it was nice for reality to pan out. And Alicia was hot.

The janitor's job was not a great start but a job. I was lucky that Alicia had been friendly enough to give me that little bit of advice. Maybe I would not have gotten that job if I had left my application as I had written it the first time. This was a department store with millions of dollars in merchandise. It was the biggest in downtown Los Angeles, and maybe they wouldn't have been quick to hire someone who had just gotten out from behind bars.

I went home, found an old brown blanket in the linen closet, and folded it over the front seat of the Chevy. I didn't want anything more critical than French fries falling straight through the car down to the street when it fell through the hole in the front seat. I tucked it in really well and considered stapling it in place.

I picked up Alicia at her small apartment on Ferguson in the City of Commerce. She shared her place with Clara, a sales clerk at Bullocks, a department store in downtown Los Angeles. I met Clara, a nine-out-of-ten.

"She has a boyfriend," Alice gave me a soft swat on my back.

"Clara, I hope you don't mind my staring—no offense intended. It's just that Alicia is stunning, and as I came here to pick her up, I definitely didn't expect to encounter another beauty queen."

Alicia and I piled in the car. I barely knew her, so I opened the car door for her, walked around to my side, and got in. "Let's go to Chinatown for dinner," I suggested. "Then we can catch a movie."

"I dig it," Alicia agreed.

"Sorry about the car," I said.

"You should see mine," she said, laughing and pointing at another rust-bucket. "It's the Pinto parked in front of my pad."

"You're just trying to make me feel good," I said.

My car had a big front seat. It stretched pretty wide. I

wouldn't say that Alicia was hugging the passenger door, but she was far over there. I extended my right hand across to her, and she took it. I slid her closer to the middle of the bench a minute later. Before long, her left arm was around my shoulders as I drove. In my head, I could hear the voices of my celibate friends back at DVI egging me on. It made me laugh a little.

"What's funny? Tell me."

"You'd never understand," I said.

"Hey, I'm not a dummy. Try me."

I laughed at her choice of words.

She laughed at me laughing at her.

The innocence at nineteen.

"How long have you been in LA?" I asked.

"I'm a lifer," she said. "How about you?"

"I got here when I was ten."

I took her to a restaurant I had been to many times before. It was probably the most excellent restaurant in Chinatown at the time. There were two floors. Everything was squeaky clean. If you wanted to eat with chopsticks, you had to ask for them, not vice versa. I needed regular silverware. I liked this place because the food and service were good, and they gave you fancy cloth napkins.

We sat across from each other.

A tiny Asian girl with long, straight hair came to the table to take our order. Her English was spoken with an attractive accent and a high-pitched voice. She was pretty, but not as pretty as Patty. A metal name tag was pinned to the tall collar of her oriental-style dress, but the writing was in Chinese.

Alicia ordered a Daiquiri. I ordered a Coke. "They don't ask for ID here," I told Alicia. "But I can't take a chance drinking alcohol. I'm on parole for a year."

"I should have ordered a Coke," she said, "I'm sorry."

"Alicia, no, I was just explaining. Drink what you want. You're not on probation."

We click her Daiquiri to my Coke in a glass.

We laughed a lot. Alicia was very laid back. Before we were halfway through dinner, it was as though we'd known each other for a long time.

By the time they brought the scoop of sherbet as dessert, Alicia had finished two large Daiquiris and did not appear to be anywhere near drunk.

"Do you want to go to the movies?" she asked me.

"I'll take you anywhere you want," I said.

Her hand was across the table. I could see a waiter at a distance watching us. I looked at her, reached over, and took her hand.

"I have my own bedroom," she said.

The smile.

One thing that stands out about Alicia is her beauty—how effortlessly direct she can be. I can't shake this feeling of familiarity mixed with something brand new. And then I find myself blushing. Me, blushing! After everything I've experienced. When she mentions her bedroom, I feel like a nine-year-old again.

"What precisely do you have in mind?"

"Have you ever played doctor with a fox like me?"

I wanted to jump out of my chair, go around the table, pick her up, squeeze her while I kissed her, and demonstrate in fine detail exactly how well I knew how to play doctor. It was how she said it.

"You're a fox, alright," I agreed. "You need to teach me about doctoring," I said.

"You should be happy I'm four years older," she said. "Just wait and see."

I remembered Christine and smiled to myself.

Our waitress arrived with a little tray that had the bill on it. I counted out the cash and put it on the tray. Technically, we were ready to leave. Alicia stood.

"Alicia, wait," I said. "I can't stand up yet."

Alicia blushed and started laughing.

Two waiters nearby started laughing, too. Alicia's laughter was infectious. I'm sure they had no idea why I couldn't get up or why she was laughing.

"Save it for me," she said.

"No, don't tell me that right now," I whispered. "I'll never get it down if you talk like that."

"Okay. Sour kraut," she said. "Dirty mop water. Running out of toilet paper. Looking down at your lunch sandwich and finding half a bug."

"Stop," I said. "Now, I'm laughing too hard to stand."

It was a great night.

After no sex for almost twenty-one months, how could it not be great? It was much too short. All I could think of was Alicia. She was so passionate. So real.

"I take the pill," she said. "Don't worry about it." I kissed her right off, and I felt a door open to her as we made love. I didn't think about Selena, Christine, Luna, Patty, or anyone else. This was about Alicia and me.

I got home at midnight. My mom and dad were both up, worried. I felt bad I had not called. It cheered them up when I told them I got a job. The department store was a block from where my Dad, Leonard, worked.

I left the house at two thirty in the morning and got to the department store twenty minutes later to start my first day of work.

* * *

After I got home from my first day on the job, my parole officer visited me.

"George, how's it going? Happy to be home?"

"Sure am. It's good to see my family again."

"Any plans?"

"I've got a job as a janitor."

"Fast work," he said.

I informed him about my employer's name, work hours, and pay rate. He took notes. Additionally, I mentioned that my parents gave me the money from selling my car after paying off the bank. I used the money to purchase a Chevy and intended to get liability insurance for it immediately.

"I see you did very well in refrigeration and air conditioning. Are you planning to pursue it?"

"My instructor at DVI said I should visit the Plumbers & Pipe Fitters Union to get on the apprentice list for refrigeration & air-conditioning. I plan to do that."

"That's good, George," he said with a slight grin. I think he was impressed. He said he'd see me in a month at his office. We shook hands, and he left.

In prison, everyone who has been on parole talks trash about parole officers. I had never been on parole or probation before. I didn't know this guy, but he seemed okay. I planned to do precisely what he expected of me. If a parole officer can handcuff you and drop you off at the county jail on any violation he believes has been committed, it is sheer stupidity not to follow the rules they give you. Pi always said being on parole is like being a dog on a short leash.

I could deal with a short leash for a year.

I picked Alicia up at home in the evening. We went out again. I didn't have to ask her to do anything. We were driving on the freeway, and she put her head in my lap. She opened my fly and took me in her mouth. It was a miracle I didn't lose control of the car.

"If I crash, it's your fault," I said, getting as comfortable as possible. In that old Chevy, there was no such thing as comfortable. I mean, we're talking about those holes in the upholstery that showed you the road under the car, and even where there weren't holes, springs were poking through.

"Hush, eyes on the road. Enjoy just as I do," she said. I felt her breath on my bare skin when she spoke, and she was working it again.

* * *

After work one day, I drove to the union to see what I needed to do to get on the apprentice list. My instructor had told me that the apprenticeship is five years long, and then you become a journeyman and can make dollars big-time. I had no idea what big-time dollars meant. I stepped into the union office and told the man behind the counter I wanted to get on the list.

"Kid, the list is so damn long; it might take years for your name to come up."

Two men were sitting at desks against a far wall, one on the phone, the other writing something. I don't think the guy was even paying attention to me, and that was like a switch for me to keep going.

"I just got released from prison, and while I was there, I got an achievement certificate for completing five hundred hours of refrigeration and air-conditioning. I got pretty good at everything I was taught. I don't mind waiting years. I hear your union is responsible for turning out journeymen who make a career out of this type of work."

One of the men came over to the counter, stretched out his hand, and I shook it. He wore a nice suit and tie, reminding me of my dad, Leonard.

"How old are you?"

"Nineteen, sir."

"How much time did you do?"

"Give or take, twenty-one months."

"Did you kill anyone or rob anyone? Was it a moral turpitude charge?"

"I pled guilty to grand theft of thirty-five hundred dollars, a loan I got under false pretenses. I also served four months in the brig for being absent without leave."

"You said your name is George."

"Yes, George Hatcher. I have my achievement certificate in this envelope."

The man took it, pulled out the document, and examined it.

"Give George an application, get a copy of this certificate, and put it on my desk," he said to the guy behind the counter, then turned to me. "George, it will take time, but I promise not years. Are you working right now?"

"Yes, sir, I am."

"Stick it out. I will call you."

"Be sure you give your phone number and a good address where we can write or call you."

"Yes, sir. Sir, I'm grateful," I said.

When I finished the application and was ready to leave, the blonde guy at the counter shook my hand and said, "We will be in touch, son."

"Thank you, sir."

The guy in a suit, the one who had listened to me, was still standing there.

"Thank you, sir." I might have shaken his hand a little too long. But it wasn't a bad thing. He was chuckling as he walked back to his desk.

I hoped it wouldn't be long before I got on the waitlist. I enjoyed doing refrigeration work. I got so good that I could easily take a compressor out of a refrigerator in the classroom, repair it, install it back, and charge it up with Freon Gas. To take the class, you had to have a drug-free record and get the approval of the teacher who interviewed all students. Freon Gas is not something you would want to sniff too much of because it will get you high, but it can also kill you.

I worked a little on air-conditioning units, but only on window units. An air-conditioner was almost like a refrigerator. It had a compressor that needed Freon to make the coil cold. The difference was there was a blower and adjustments, and both had a temperature control. The union scale for a starting apprentice was about four dollars[1] an hour. That was a bunch of money then. My janitor's job was paying me about $1.25 an hour. For a week or so, I was on edge, actively waiting. I thought I'd get a call fast, but I stopped sweating it. It was like that old saying about a watched pot never boiling. I knew I had to get over it and keep busy, and eventually, the phone would ring. My gut told me the guy at the desk would get me in.

* * *

---

[1]. $4.00 in 1962 equates to $34.26 in 2020

My days fell into a routine. I worked from three until noon and went home to sleep. At seven, I picked up Alicia, and we went out. Sometimes, we stayed at her apartment, locked up in her bedroom. If her roommate happened to be there, she'd joke around.

"Save some for me."

"I have enough for both of you," I said.

For the longest time since discovering Selena's infidelity with Sergio, I had wondered if Selena loved both of us.

Alicia would lead me towards the bedroom. "You don't have enough for both of us. Stop flirting."

Clara was hot, maybe a year older than Alicia. They both looked my age or younger. I wanted them both. Was that what Selena wanted? She wanted me, and she wanted Sergio?

Alicia and I drove to the mountains or beach on the weekend and had a great time. We spent very little money. You can't spend it if you don't have it. When I worked at the drugstore, I spent so much money in the same spots I was now visiting with Alicia.

If I had only tried harder and not blown the drugstore money, I could have paid Thelma. What would my life look like if I hadn't gone to DVI? I would have stayed in the Navy and the medical field, maybe. I'm not smart enough to be a doctor, but if the Thelma repayment fiasco had not happened, I would not have ended up locked up.

Looking back on the 'what if' is a bitch.

Chapter 2
The Locker Thing

"I think we should be exclusive," I suggested. Alicia chuckled softly. "That's the age gap talking," she replied with a smirk. "We're together every day. Isn't that exclusive enough?"

"Okay, I get it," I said, conceding to her point. My thoughts drifted to my ex-wife, Selena. Before we tied the knot, I nagged her relentlessly about marriage, and she had said the same thing. I pushed her until she finally agreed, but it all fell apart soon after.

One evening, after dining at our preferred eatery in Chinatown, we decided to catch a movie. Alicia drew my attention to a woman's white handbag. "It's crafted from lizard skin," she informed me.

"Stunning," I responded, attempting to feign interest. "I'll purchase one for you." "They're priced at a hundred and fifty dollars."

"That's fine," I assured her, secretly hoping she would let it slide.

"We have them at the store," she mentioned, feeding me

popcorn from a large tub. "I know a way you could get the bag without spending a dime," she suggested.

"I'd have to steal it," I assumed.

"No, I'll do the stealing," she corrected me. "All you need to do is stash it in a customer locker on the mezzanine during the night."

"Then what happens?"

"You hand me the locker key while we're both at work, and I'll handle the rest."

I turned to face her. She was gazing at the screen, her beautiful face illuminated by the technicolor light. Her perfume, complex and luxurious, filled my nostrils, likely a product from the perfume section. The situation was eerily similar to when I discovered Christine was skimming from the cash register, leading us to become accomplices. I never served time for that particular theft, but I felt my time in prison was retribution for all my past illegal activities. (Rationalizing.)

"You're serious about this, aren't you?" I asked.

When she smiled, her teeth sparkled in the light from the screen. "I never utter words I don't mean," she affirmed.

Luna had said the same thing, but Luna never enticed me to steal anything.

Alicia expected an argument from me, but I surprised both of us.

Reflecting on it now, I am astounded by my own recklessness to jeopardize my freedom and risk a return to incarceration for parole violation and potentially a charge of grand theft.

"Give me a step-by-step, and I'll do it," I said.

"I don't want to pressure you."

"You aren't pressuring me," I said. "Like you said, you're doing the stealing. I'm not taking the purse out of the store. You are."

I heard a muffled giggle. "Are you sure you're only nineteen?"

Alicia's bright smile stood out eerily in the dim theater. The space was grand, adorned with opulent red velvet curtains covering almost every surface but the ceiling, floor, and aisle. The place was packed with people, and we were encircled by hushed whispers. The individuals behind us were busy shushing others. A man on our row had an uncontrollable hyena-like laugh at inappropriate moments, while a teenager in the middle had made several trips to the concession stand, even accidentally spilling a large orange soft drink on my shoes once. The row ahead of us was in constant chatter, and somewhere in the theater, a baby was wailing. Amidst all this commotion, Alicia chose this chaotic setting to share her plans. It might not have been the most suitable place, but that's where it all unfolded.

The janitors I worked with were friendly, although I hadn't worked there long enough to know any of them very well. None were younger than forty. Most were over sixty. They seemed trusting of one another, particularly of me, maybe because I reminded them of a son or something. Everyone had relatives I reminded them of.

At three in the morning, fifteen janitors clocked in when I did. My job was to clean the buyers' offices on the mezzanine floor. Where I worked, all the overhead lights were on. On the merchandise floors, a janitor would turn off the lights in an area he had just cleaned and on in the next area to be cleaned. A sales floor was never fully illuminated. It was easy to move around without being seen from afar. The store was huge.

The first floor where the purse was located was a long way from the mezzanine floor office area I was assigned to. For two days, I observed who worked where. I made it a point to get friendly with the two janitors on the first floor and went to shoot the breeze with them while they were working. It was not uncommon for a janitor to leave his area to shoot the breeze in another area.

It was a tight group. I wasn't in any of the cliques, but I was well-treated by everyone, including our immediate boss, Mr. Lewis, who arrived when we were ready to end our shift.

On the third night, I put the lizard purse in a shopping bag in one of the customer lockers. A nickel in the slot allowed me to remove the key. It was so quick and easy that I went back and took another purse in a different color.

After the store opened, I used a payphone to call Alicia at her desk.

"Hi, it's me."

"What's happening?"

"The locker key is in the ashtray of my car across the street." I heard her breathing quicken. "The car is unlocked, so lock it up afterward, okay?"

"Okay." I heard a sigh. "George?"

"Yeah?"

"I can't wait to see you tonight. Let's get a pizza and stay in."

"Can we buy the extra-large in case Clara is around?" I wasn't joking.

"You're a flirt. You won't let go."

"I'm not a flirt. I'm just a man with a big ...appetite."

Alicia laughed. I pictured her at her desk. I loved her laugh.

I arrived at her house that night with an extra-large pizza and three extra-large drinks. Both of them were at the door when I got there. I couldn't remember the last time I had been hugged and kissed by two women at the same time. Alicia hadn't told me that she had given Clara one of the purses.

Alicia was older than me, but I'm not so sure she'd ever been in a threesome. I'd never been in one except in my imagination. I had thumbed through a lot of X-rated magazines with threesomes, foursomes, and free-for-all melees with too many bodies to count. I asked myself, again, is this what Selena wanted, both of us?

We drank from the sodas using a straw while engaged or doing something nasty to each other, but we didn't touch the pizza until after two hours of sex on Alicia's bed. Look, if you're ever in a threesome, you're never going to forget the first time. If I wrote everything that happened, my editor would give my story a five X rating. I'll leave the specifics to your imagination.

At work, I never went to Alicia's office or met her in the store or nearby. My hours were crazy early, and I was gone way before noon. I clocked out at eleven-thirty.

"Get some cool stuff for you," Alicia urged. "It will be here when you come over."

"Sounds like you are looking for something new," I teased, knowing her like I did by now.

"No, no, I'm thinking of you."

We laughed.

I acted impulsively on each occasion, and those choices were mine to make. I don't want you to believe that Alicia was responsible for my actions; she just happened to be older.

I'd gone to school with kids who bragged about shoplifting, and I never stooped to doing it. My parents didn't teach me to steal. Still, I did worse and paid the price for it. This newfound scheme involving a locker, which soon escalated to multiple lockers, was fraught with risk and utterly immoral. I should have paused to contemplate my actions. Instead, my mind was consumed by carnal desires.

* * *

One morning before I checked out, Mr. Lewis called me in his office. That caused me a heart attack and a half, but all he told me was that the buyer's office manager said that everyone was happy about how clean their offices were being kept.

I went beyond what the guy who trained me told me to do, which was vacuum and throw out the trash in each office, period. I did that and cleaned the desks, taking special care in putting files back the way they were. Pledge left a clean scent that told the occupant I had been there. I cleaned the hanging overhead fluorescent lights that hung on chains over some desks. I did this because I had the time to do it, and I figured if I was a janitor, I had to be a good janitor. That was important to me. I should have thought more about how I was being a thief janitor.

* * *

I made mental notes of what Alicia wanted and started getting something for myself. How many khakis does a guy need? I went for jeans, then sporty stuff, expensive shirts, shoes.

Alicia was crazy about shoes. The trick was getting her size. I would have to write an entire chapter explaining how I figured out how the sizes are kept in the stock room and how to match what is on display in the dark.

Clara, who worked at Bullocks, three blocks away, started helping Alicia out. Clara would get the locker key. The department store was filled with employees and customers, and no one noticed Clara or Alicia come into the customer service area where lines of people were returning something or buying a gift certificate. Clara or Alicia would walk through the crowds to a locker and carry out the bags like they were purchases they had made. This was before alert tags on clothing that would set off an alarm when you exited. However, if there had been such a gadget, we would have figured out how to disable it.

When I got home from Alicia's every night, it was late. I'd lie on my bed until it was time to leave for work. Bedtime was when I got home, about noon. When I was alone, I did have guilt trips. I was pissed at myself for doing what I was doing. My mom hardly went into my room. I made my own bed and did my own laundry. When mom asked me about the clothes I wore, I told her I got great discounts. I had jeans to spare. At one point, I told Alicia and Clara to keep the men's stuff I had taken and sell it. Every day I kept thinking the union people would be in touch with me.

To clarify, I am not suggesting that my actions were a result of being influenced by two women who were four and five years older than me. I would be turning twenty in October, but I was behaving as if I was thirty. After Juarez, the Navy, and the subsequent events, I should have been well-versed in risky business. However, I was so deeply engrossed in my relationships with Alicia and Clara that I failed to consider the potential consequences of my actions.

Occasionally, I contemplated reaching out to Luna, but I never made the call. In my moments of weakness, I never contacted Patty again after that one time. I didn't even inquire about her living situation, whether she was still residing at home with her mother and brother.

* * *

In the dim light of the evening, I found myself standing before Alicia's apartment, only to be confronted by a man I never met before. His words were laced with hostility, "You're messing with my girl, ese. I'm going to make you pay," he threatened.

We stood a mere ten feet from the apartment's entrance, our feet sinking into the small patch of grass beneath us. He jabbed his index finger into my chest, a gesture meant to intimidate me. What he did was piss me off. As a child, I admired Pi's muscular physique and his ability to withstand punches to his chest without so much as a flinch. He had taught me how to hold my own.

Yet, this stranger's audacity to poke me with his finger ignited a spark of anger within me. He was larger in size, but it didn't matter. Fear was a foreign concept to me. I retaliated, my fist connecting with his jaw, the sound of the impact echoing in the night.

At that moment, Alicia and Clara arrived on the scene as he collapsed to the ground, his face streaked with tears. Clara, displaying concern for her boyfriend, promptly drove him to the nearest hospital, where he received treatment for a fractured jaw. It was then that I discovered his name was Danny. The unexpected turn of events was that Danny was, in fact, Clara's boyfriend, not Alicia's. Following that night, Danny never had the courage to encounter me again.

Soon after the incident, I felt bad that I hurt him. I wanted to apologize when I ran into him at the apartment with Clara, but I couldn't.

I said to Alicia, "Fix Danny up with some stuff from the locker thing, whatever he wants."

"I got some fabulous shades to start with," Alicia said. "I'll see what he wants."

George J Hatcher

* * *

One evening, in Danny's absence, Clara decided to visit Alicia's room. She found us lounging on the bed, engrossed in a television show. Without hesitation, she asked, "May I join you?" even as she was already making her way towards us.

Alicia responded in a playful tone, "You're welcome to join us, but you only get to watch TV with us. I don't want any more drama between George and Danny."

I agreed wholeheartedly, "Absolutely," I said, extending my hand towards Clara, who had already settled on the bed.

Clara retorted, "I'm not married, I can fuck anyone I want."

"Does Danny know that?" I asked.

Eyes went from the television to Clara.

"If he plays the jealous bullshit again, I told him already, we're done."

"Does Danny know you do it with us?" I was asking the questions.

"He doesn't have to know," Clara said.

The bond between the three of us was profound, transcending mere physical attraction. As for what you might have been doing at our age in 1962, it's likely you were also exploring your own relationships and sexuality. We had a strong bond and enjoyed each other's company. Instead of going out often, Alicia and I spent a lot of time at the apartment, watching TV, being intimate, and planning our next shopping trip. I considered moving in with them, but I couldn't do so without permission from my parole officer.

It was just as well. At my parents' house, I had a big room all to myself, and I really enjoyed the spectacular view from the balcony off the living room that overlooked all of downtown Los Angeles. I often sat out there to eat lunch-take-out before I hit the sack. At night, I was at Alicia and Clara's pad. I loved being with them, but I really wanted out of the janitor job and the locker thing.

* * *

In the early hours of the morning, my shopping adventures began to branch out into other departments. While jewelry was securely locked away, items like colognes, perfumes, sporting goods, and many more were not. It was a thrill that bordered on recklessness.

However, as time went on, the thrill began to fade for me. The act of stealing just for the sake of it started to feel wrong. Without the necessity, the risk, the adrenaline rush, the act lost its allure. The thrill of stealing was replaced by a dull monotony when it was done safely. Perhaps I was trying to justify my wrongdoings. It felt as though I was compensating for my thefts by risking getting caught. If the risk was eliminated, then it felt like I wasn't really paying the price. My thought process was as chaotic and irrational as my actions.

Alicia and Clara were living a life similar to mine. They retained only a fraction of what came through those lockers. I would often jest about them being the local fences. I never dipped my toes into the selling aspect, and I was oblivious to the details of their transactions. Both of them were day workers and night revelers. I was left wondering when they found the time to sell.

My job and the thrill of theft had lost their charm for me. I found myself daydreaming about the job that the union promised me. Looking back, I must have been oblivious to the risks I had been taking. It was hard to believe that I had actually gone through with it all, especially considering I was on parole. It's been so long I can't say for sure.

George J Hatcher

* * *

I was comfortably settled at home, enjoying an early dinner, when I discovered a letter addressed to me. As I sat on my balcony, taking in the view of Los Angeles and savoring my take-out meal, I began to read the letter. It was from Lily, a union representative who had made several unsuccessful attempts to reach me by phone. The letter instructed me to contact the union and specifically ask for Lily. The reason? A job interview was waiting for me.

Without wasting any time, I dialed her number, which led to an interview with the manager of WESPAC. This company specialized in commercial installations of HVAC systems, including Heating and air conditioning. They also manufactured and installed galvanized steel ductwork.

By Wednesday, I was hired, and by the following Monday, I was meeting the general manager at the WESPAC office at seven in the morning. The ductwork tubes were massive, resembling tunnels, likely designed for large buildings. I was eager to learn more.

The manager, Hank, explained, "Our work spans from inception to completion. We handle commercial stores, shopping centers, universities, and more." The union had informed him about my past in Youth Authority Confinement, which I referred to as prison.

Hank assured me, "You don't need any tools. We have everything here. We don't provide uniforms, but the journeyman you'll be assigned to will guide you on the appropriate attire."

I was then given a tour of the expansive plant, the factory where sheet metal was produced, and the ductwork customized for ongoing projects. My experience with a refrigerator and window unit was modest, but I had a grasp on the thermodynamics of how a gas like Freon, under extreme pressure, could cause temperature changes. As part of the apprenticeship program, I was required to attend trade tech school for two hours in the evening twice a month.

* * *

I apologized to Mr. Lewis at work that I couldn't give more notice but that this was a great opportunity for me, and they had tried to reach me for a week on the phone.

"You've done very good work, George. I am happy for you. Janitor work is not what you were cut out to do."

"I didn't mind," I said. "It was a pleasure, sir," I said, shaking his hand.

Chapter 3
My New Job

In the cozy comfort of Alicia and Clara's apartment, we were nestled in bed like a trio of contented campers. The air was fragrant, adding to the homely atmosphere. That particular night, I had plans to take Alicia out, but she insisted that we all stay in.

There we were, the three of us comfortably propped against the headboard with the television humming softly in the background. I found myself sandwiched in the middle. We were all dressed in matching sporty gray sweats, a generous gift from the local department store.

"I want you to know it's not like I'm disappearing forever," I reassured Alicia.

"Well, it's not like we spent much time together at work," she retorted.

In a playful tone, I suggested, "Maybe you should consider not hiring a replacement. Quit while you're ahead."

Clara chuckled at this, asking, "So, you're aware then?"

"Aware of what?" I questioned.

Alicia said, "She's about to tell you that I've always had this fantasy about the locker thing, but I never had a partner in crime. When I learned about your past, I assured you that the only opportunity was in the janitor's department."

It took a moment for the penny to drop. I turned to look at Alicia, her face adorned with a wide grin as if this was all a big joke. For a moment, I felt a pang of betrayal. I had suffered through a hellish time behind bars due to my past mistakes, and she had used my tarnished history to get me through the door when all I wanted was a fresh start. But I quickly brushed off the resentment. The job was a thing of the past. I had learned to let things slide a long time ago. I joined in their laughter. Since my release, Alicia has been my closest friend, with Clara not far behind. I held a deep affection for them both.

"Telling me only the janitor department had an opening is going to cost you," I playfully warned, engaging in a friendly tussle with Alicia and then with both of them.

"From the moment you first spoke, even before I shredded your application, I was drawn to you. I liked you before you became the locker candidate and before I knew about your past incarceration," Alicia confessed.

Clara, unable to contain her laughter, chimed in, "She's trying to clean up being found out."

"Quiet, you," Alicia retorted, playfully assaulting her with a pillow.

Our wrestling match ended, and we settled back onto the bed.

"It's alright. It's been an incredible journey," I reassured them.

"Who gives you better advice than me?" Alicia asked rhetorically.

"Clara isn't too shabby," I countered. The look on Alicia's face was priceless.

Wham! I was the recipient of a pillow attack. Throughout

our time together, we had shared so many joyful moments that I was convinced our friendship would stand the test of time. It's a bittersweet reality of life that it often intervenes, pulling those we consider lifelong friends out of our lives. Patty was once my 'forever friend,' but now we had lost touch. I was grateful to Alicia for bringing me into their world and helping me secure that job, but I could feel the winds of change blowing once again.

No more department store.
No more early morning shifts.
No more afternoon naps.

On Monday, I started a new job with a high salary, much more than I earned as a janitor. This didn't include the extra money I made from the "four-finger discount" profits. If I didn't gain weight, I wouldn't need to buy new clothes for a long time. I had so many pairs of tennis shoes that it was embarrassing.

I was assigned to a journeyman named Matt. He wasn't just a bit shorter than me; he was significantly so, and at 55, he was a good deal older than my 20 years. I would quickly learn that Matt was a paradox of a man - mean yet funny, stern yet engaging. He was a constant figure in his cap and glasses, the latter of which he had a habit of throwing in fits of frustration.

Matt and I worked on what he called the rough installs. My first day on the job was his first day on the site of a Thrifty Drugstore in construction. When we finished this job, the installation was ready for startup. The startup crew would come in after us, charge the systems with Freon, start the compressors and cooling towers, and calibrate the airflow needed for each opening in the store. Dampers inside the ducts are controlled by small motors to open or close, depending on how much air is required for each register where the air comes into the store.

I had a small portable Motorola radio that had great sound. I took it to work, thinking I could listen to my favorite station while working.

I set it down on the rooftop and turned it on while we were setting up.

Matt turned on me like I'd done something wild, like, I don't know, pee off a roof or something.

"Take that thing to your car and lock it up," he said, frowning at me. "Right now. Drop what you're doing."

Neil Sedaka was playing. I wanted to listen to the song's end, so it was on while carrying it.

Like a mind-reader, he said, "And turn it off. Right now."

It took a few minutes to get down to the first floor, but I returned fast. I got the lecture to end all lectures. Matt went bananas on me and told me never to bring a radio to a job.

"Music is distracting. I don't want you hurting yourself or hurting both of us."

This job was important to me. I let it go. I had a radio in my car and blasted it while driving.

Matt, the journeyman, was the biggest grump you would never want to meet. From the beginning, I made up my mind that I would win him over with hard work and determination. He wasted no time teaching me to weld. In those days, we used silver floss to join copper tubing. The copper pipe runs were each twenty feet long, and sometimes, it took more than twenty of these heavy mothers to be welded together. This is what the freon gas would eventually flow through.

Matt was thin but rugged and sweated up a storm. His glasses would fog up, blocking his vision. Sometimes he got so pissed off that he'd throw his glasses aside. Sometimes, they would break. I was always running to the truck to get him an extra pair.

It was always, "What took you so damn long?"

"Next time, I'll do it in record time," I'd say.

He would grunt. When Matt grunted, it was a sign of approval.

One time, the crane loaded equipment on the roof of a Thrifty Drugstore when Matt and I were not there, and they placed the unit about a hundred feet from where the plans called for it to be. Matt cussed up a storm, threw his cap down, and kicked it; then he started to throw his glasses. I offered to hold them for him.

He didn't like that.

"So, what do we do now, call the crane company?" I asked. I didn't know we were going to move the pyramids.

He had me get the odds and ends of galvanized pipes from the truck and bring them to the roof.

"Make sure the pipes are at least six feet long."

I went down our ladder to the parking lot level and had to carry the pipes up one at a time while Matt waited impatiently. Once five were up there, he took a long crowbar, a 4X4 piece of wood, and a 2X4 and shimmed them under the wood frame that housed the huge compressor that weighed at least eight hundred pounds.

"Now, you get ready with that pipe. As soon as I get it up a little, see if you can push the pipe under, but don't stand behind it in case it pops back. I got no time to run you to the hospital."

"Got it, Matt. No worries."

We could easily push the monster after we had three pipes beneath the crate. Each time we advanced a bit, I ran to put another pipe at the front. Then, we pushed some more. It took a while. When we got to the unit where it was supposed to be, I looked at it in amazement. I was in awe of Matt.

"The new gravel roof is going to need repair," I said, looking back at where the compressor had been.

"Fuck it. More work for the roofer," he said.

"Okay, Hatcher. Start taking the frame off," he said.

There was no rest. While he did his measuring and layout, I pried the wood away from the unit. When I was done, I got my first look at the compressor's actual size—a monster version of the tiny compressors I used to work on back at DVI that came out of a refrigerator or a window unit air conditioning.

Matt was known to do WESPAC installs in record time. We did my first Thrifty Store in seven working days. He complained that we could have done it in six days if not for the unit being put in the wrong spot. I don't think so because moving the monster only took a couple of hours, but I nodded in agreement.

When we started a second Thrifty Store, he handed me an envelope with three hundred dollars.

"I get a bonus when I bring in a job fast. You're a good worker, Hatcher, and you learn quickly."

Surprised and happy, he walked away before I could thank him. That's how Matt was. WESPAC had a contract to do twenty-one Thrifty Stores, back-to-back. I wondered if Matt would do all of them and if I would get a bonus every time he did. I was all proud of the bonus; it was legit money.

A few days after we finished the first Thrifty, I was discharged from parole. They cut me loose after nine months instead of a year. The parole officer sent me a discharge letter in which he wrote, "I wish you the best of luck, George. Keep moving forward like you are doing."

Guilt trips should have straightened my brain out. At that point in my life, I carried two sins. The drugstore thing with Christine and the Locker Thing. It was 1962.

Chapter 4
The Double Life: Balancing Work, Love, and Fun

I commenced my studies at Los Angeles Trade Tech in the bustling downtown area. This educational setting contrasted sharply with my previous experiences. At Los Angeles Trade Tech, my classmates were unfamiliar individuals, predominantly older than me and coming from diverse backgrounds. The course was brief, yet the subject matter was complex. I made a conscious effort to stay attentive. As the instructor began using tangible demonstrations, like boiling water, to illustrate the boiling point and its correlation to the gas flow through the copper pipes Matt and I were welding, the material began to coalesce into a comprehensible whole. The extensive 500 hours I had invested in refrigeration and air conditioning at DVI proved invaluable.

* * *

When I didn't wear gloves to weld and got burned at work, Matt would scream at me from wherever he was. He had ears like an elephant.

"That's what you get!"

No matter what, I held a great deal of admiration for Matt; I honestly looked up to him. He was brilliant. One of the first things I did on a new job was set up a folding drafting table, usually on the roof, where most of our work took place. No chairs or stools were available, so Matt would take a two-by-four and nail two pieces together to create a "T" for the tabletop to rest on. He would then prop the job plans on the table.

* * *

In a couple of days of working from the architect's plans for the job we were on, I got the hang of it. I caught him smiling a few times.

"Take the measurements off the plans and lay it out," he said.

"Consider it done," I said like I was an expert.

"You're getting pretty darn good at this," Matt said. A rare compliment that I ate up.

* * *

When I started working with Matt, he ate his lunch in the truck, and I ate my lunch up on the roof. When we were on the third job at another Thrifty, he invited me to join him in the truck.

"It's none of my business," he said as he chewed on a sandwich. "You don't need to tell me."

"You mean about the twenty-one months I did in prison?"

"Yeah. That's a long time, man. And you are just a youngster."

I told him part of it that day and continued for a few more days. By the time I finished, he knew about Juarez, the brig, the money from Thelma, and how the judge kicked my ass. What I told him is what is pretty much on record. I didn't tell him about the drugstore swiping or the fake letters. Those actions remain embarrassing to me, even decades later.

"Kid, you're going to do good in this trade."

He would always be grumpy, and he would always scream and get pissed off, but that's how he was.

He was very kind to me, and even though I didn't always receive a bonus, he gave me a bonus of five hundred dollars after we completed a challenging supermarket job that took two long weeks. While the bonuses were appreciated, I was especially thrilled with the paychecks I received.

I'm sure that the owners of WESPAC put up with him because he was so good at his job.

I'd hear him screaming on a payphone when he'd call dispatch at WESPAC to complain about the wrong delivered material or essential parts not being sent. When that happened, I could predict what he would say to the person on the other end.

"Now you get those fucking pipes over here by sunrise tomorrow, or I'll have your ass fired. Got it?" followed by, "Look, I want to finish this job. I'm sure you want a paycheck next payday, right?"

WESPAC had a lot of employees, but Matt talked like he was the one and only. In my eyes, he was Superman.

As for my personal life, I was exhausted. I was lucky I was still at my parents' place because I didn't have enough energy to come home and cook. To be clear, I never cooked before. I didn't have to shop for groceries or cook meals at my parents' house. By the time I got home and took a shower, I was feeling beat up. I would have dinner and just enough energy to get to my room to lie down, watch television, and talk to Alicia and sometimes Clara.

"You are treating me like my pussy smells," Alicia said.

"I just got hard," I said.

I could hear Clara in the background, laughing.

"Nonsense. You have the sweetest pussy I have ever had."

"And me?" I heard Clara say.

"Goes for both of you. I'm just dead tired. I work for a crazy workhorse."

"You should have stayed at the store," Alicia said.

"Yeah, right." My turn to laugh first.

* * *

Two days later, as soon as I walked through the door, I got a call from Alicia. She was crying. I moved to the phone in my room and started pulling off my dirty work clothes as we talked.

"What's wrong?"

"I got fired today," she said.

"Were you stealing?"

"Don't be a retard. No, I didn't steal anything."

"How can they fire you? For what? You run the department." I sat on my bed to pull off my socks and toss them in the basket.

"I don't run the department. My boss in the back office runs the department."

She had been warned about using the phone too much and had three written warnings.

"I been there three years, and it didn't matter to my bitch boss. She gave me a lousy week of severance pay and dumped me right on the spot."

I dug a set of gray sweats out of my drawer to put on after my shower. I still had a stack of unopened sweats in a box in my closet. I lay back on the bed and stretched out. I was stripped down to my boxers, and the ceiling fan over my bed was higher than it should have been, blasting me with a refreshing breeze. I could hear Alicia still crying on the phone.

She stopped crying and said, "If you were still working there, we could have continued the locker thing. I could still go in there and get what you left in the locker."

"Alicia, get serious. We're lucky it went on so long without a hitch.

* * *

When I got home the next day, she called and told me, "I'm having trouble getting over getting fired."

"I'm coming over to see you as soon as I shower."

"Shower here after you fuck me. I'm so upset. I need the release. Hurry."

I hadn't seen her in at least a week, and suddenly, I was hurting to see her. I told my mom I had to leave. I skipped dinner, put away the sweats, put on a pair of the clean gray khakis I wore to work, fresh socks, and tennis shoes, and went to see her.

Clara was out, so the two of us were there.

* * *

"I want it hard right here," she said. "After, I'll blow you like never before."

As the front door shut, we were out of our clothes and going at each other like a couple of hungry animals. I was on top, and she wrapped her legs around me, and we both exploded right there on the carpet, not two feet from the sofa.

We rolled over on our backs, stared at the ceiling, and caught our breath for a minute before bundling up our clothes and heading into Alicia's bedroom. Her room had a small, unimpressive window looking out at her apartment complex, but it was covered by nice drapes that matched the garden scene on her bedspread and pillows. You know where she got that set. I hung my stuff over the easy chair in her room.

"Where's Clara?"

"Stop worrying about her. Don't you have enough with me?" Alicia said, sitting up on her bed.

I sat beside her, bunching pillows at my back.

"Hey, if Clara still has her job, that's something. I'll help you out, you know that."

"I'm not broke," she said. "I have about two thousand in the bank, but it won't last long. I got to find another job. I wish she hadn't fired me."

"Stop sweating your job. Your boss did you a favor. Now you can get something better where you don't have to work in a box."

"Are you saying my office was a box?"

"Yeah, a brown wood box, a mini library with no books."

"You fucker."

She punched my shoulder with the heel of her hand.

"I'm ready when you are," I said.

"You should be ready. It only took you five minutes to pop."

"Fuck, I hate that word pop," I said. "You should know I can go more than an hour."

We were both sitting up against the headboard. She rolled over, straddling my lap.

"Okay, I won't say pop to you anymore. I see you're ready."

She didn't have to guide it in. It knew the way.

"Hey, what about my shower?"

"Shh. Concentrate. Hard, you know, hard."

* * *

After we were spent, we stayed in bed and talked. "If Clara is at work and you're at work, who do you talk to so much on the phone?"

"I have friends I talk to at their work, friends who don't have a job. My office is not busy. I get bored. The phone is like taking a break. Was, past tense."

"You said you had three warnings in writing. Was that over the whole three-year period you were there?"

"What are you, a cop or something?" She didn't laugh. She looked away.

I hadn't really been curious, but after her actions, I felt like she was hiding something. I shrugged. "I'm curious. No big deal."

"Not the whole three years. I got written up these last six months."

"Who do you talk to so much?"

Now, I was curious.

She sat up on the bed. I sat up on the bed and faced her. She had evasion written all over her.

"If you want to know my ex-boyfriend. He's been out of work for months."

"Okay, that makes more sense," I said.

I felt sure she wasn't thinking of another dude when we were together. Her eyes were set on mine, always. If she was fantasizing, would she have her eyes closed? She never called me by another name. And it was me she called to come over. I didn't ask if she had called him first.

Maybe I could have spent the night. I drove home and thought about Alicia and me. She had never mentioned an ex-boyfriend. A hot girl like her, I would be surprised if there was only one boyfriend. Was the boyfriend still in the picture? Was this going to be another Sergio?

Why can't I be content with two women and keep my mind off the ex-boyfriend? Fuck it. Nothing lasts forever. My first wife told me that as her parting words.

Chapter 5
Driven by Determination and Entrepreneurial Spirit

A's I was driving down the street, I noticed a shiny metallic blue Impala that immediately caught my attention. I decided to pull into the Chevrolet dealer on Atlantic Boulevard in East Los Angeles on a sunny Saturday morning to take a closer look. There it was, looking impressive with a price tag of two thousand nine hundred, fully loaded. I wasn't exactly sure what "fully loaded" meant, but I was determined to find out.

I had about a thousand dollars in the bank, mainly from bonuses Matt had given me. If I was going to buy this new car, I needed a bank to finance me with a small down payment.

During my elementary school years, I was always on the lookout for ways to earn money. This entrepreneurial spirit was evident even before I moved from Douglas, Arizona, a story I detailed in Book One of this series. I was around eight when I landed my first job delivering newspapers.

I got a newspaper job after moving to Los Angeles at age 10. When that ended, I found a new venture. I began doing gardening work after school and on weekends. My friend Pi was my partner in this endeavor. Despite him being my partner, I received a larger share of the profits. This was because the business was my idea, and I owned all our gardening tools.

I can't recall when I opened my Bank of America account, but I know it was during my gardening days. Then, I met Mr. Holmberg, a banker at the branch. We became friends, perhaps because he had a son my age. When I bought my first car, I paid half the money upfront, and Mr. Holmberg arranged a car loan to finance the other half. I was only sixteen. My stepdad signed for me.

When I was sent to prison, I had to ask my father, Leonard, to sell the car and settle the remaining bank debt. He did as I asked, and there was money left over. He gave this to me upon my release.

I went to see Mr. Holmberg and spent at least five minutes telling him about my apprentice job and the future I saw for myself when I became a journeyman. He never mentioned the prison time I did; he was just the coolest as he always was with me.

"I don't want to bother my parents about signing for me. I saw this car for just under three thousand, and the problem is I don't have the money in the bank like I used to have to put a big down payment. Can you help me, or should I wait?" (I was 20 years old)

He actually snapped his fingers before he spoke, showing me a smile. "I'm proud of you, George. You have more grit than anyone I know. I'll make the car loan. You don't need your parents to sign."

* * *

I parked at a distance so construction debris wouldn't get on my car. When Matt saw it, he wasn't thrilled.

"What are you, crazy or what? You make a few dollars and then buy a new car. What was wrong with the one you had?"

"Matt, every day for months, I've been thinking my clunker was on its last wheels. It just refused to die. I had to get this baby."

"Car looked good to me. It ran. The inside was like new."

"Thanks to an upholstery shop owner who gave me a deal. You could see straight through to the street when I brought it in, and springs were coming up through the fabric."

'Not any of my damn business anyhow," he said.

"Hey Matt, thanks to you, I can afford it."

He grunted.

"Let's hit it. We're ten minutes late."

I would look down from the roof at my car at every chance. I was so happy it made me horny.

I visited Alicia that night.

I parked at the curb in front of her apartment, where I always parked. The street she lived on, Ferguson, was very commercial, but her apartment had several buildings. Alicia was almost over the job loss, or so it seemed. She came out to my car and sat in it, inhaling deeply.

"The smell is a turn-on. Let's break in the back seat?"

"You mean here?"

"Fuckin A, I mean right here," she said.

We did it and then went inside her apartment. This reminded me of Luna and me on the night she smuggled me back to the USA from Mexico and the intimate moments we shared in the back seat of her dad's Ford, which was smaller than my new car.

"How did you swing the car loan?" Carla asked.

"I've known the banker for years. When my mom married

my stepdad, I got them a loan from the same banker to buy their first car. Later, when they bought a house, his bank loaned my parents the money to swing the buy."

Alicia said, "You have so many stories to tell; you're amazing."

"Aw shucks," I joked.

"Let's take a trip somewhere," Carla suggested.

"Can we?" she looked at me eagerly, much like a child wanting to go to Disneyland. But what would I know about that kind of look?

* * *

We were in the den on the couch. A couple of take-out plates from our favorite Chinese place were half-eaten on the coffee table beside our beers. Alicia hugged me. When we kissed, the taste of beer in our mouths was an aphrodisiac to me.

"My ex-boyfriend wanted to get married," she said. "I didn't want to, and he told me to fuck off. Then he lost his job and started calling me at work. I told him I was committed."

"You told him that?"

"Fuckin A."

"I thought we weren't going steady," I said to be funny.

"Stop right there. Not that again."

I laughed. Alicia didn't.

"You want me to get married, don't you? I didn't think you wanted anything like that."

"I didn't," she said.

"Didn't? You changed your mind?"

She looked down, blushing faintly. She didn't need to say she'd changed her mind. I could see it in her face.

"I'd marry you," I said. "I'm just not financially ready yet. I will be, though. This job I have is dynamite."

She kissed me harder. By harder, I mean teeth meet teeth, tongues played, and hands roamed.

"Let's get married," Alicia said. "I loved you since the day I saw you."

We pulled apart to look at each other, both breathing heavily.

"You already know I did, too," I said. "If I sound hesitant, it's because I was married before. It happened quick and look at how it ended."

"I'm not Selena. Don't compare me to that woman who used you. She was in love with the boyfriend all along."

"I never told you that," I said. "I don't believe that's what happened."

"I don't want to discuss her," Alicia said.

We didn't talk any more about marriage that night. We just moved into the bedroom and fucked our brains out. When Clara got home, she must have heard. She knocked on the door.

Alicia stopped what she was doing and asked, "You want her in here with us?"

"Not now," I said. "Don't stop."

"Good answer," she said, biting me lightly.

Chapter 6
Ensenada, Mexico

The following weekend, a trip to Ensenada, a quaint city nestled in Baja California, Mexico, known for its vibrant nightlife and myriad of entertainment options. The plan was to stay overnight, an exciting prospect, especially since I was eager to take my new car for a long spin. The route to Baja would inevitably lead us through Tijuana, a city that held a bitter memory of a jail cell I was desperate to forget. Our destination was Ensenada, and I intended to traverse Tijuana as swiftly as possible.

When I arrived at Alicia's early, I noticed that Danny's car was in the parking lot. Maybe he had spent the night. Maybe he does what I do when he's not around and fucks both of them.

Did I really care? Yes, I did.

Alicia came out of the apartment and met me outside. She kissed me. I put my arm around her waist, brought her close, and kissed her back.

"Big favor," she says. "Clara and Danny want to go with us."

"You got to be kidding. Clara's okay, but not Danny."

"Baby, please. I'll give you the best sex ever, please."

I gave in fast.

"They get their own room, and they pay their own way," I said.

"Of course."

It didn't matter how much I liked being with Clara and Alicia. I wasn't ready to share a room with another couple.

When Danny and Clara were in the back seat with their sunglasses on, Danny said, "Hey George, thanks for letting us come along. You're chill."

"No problem," I said.

I remember when they wired his mouth. I owed him. I knew I could piss him off with a word. What would he do if I told him I'd seen every birthmark on Clara's body? I bet that would unleash Danny's wrath. I chucked.

"What's funny?" Alicia wanted to know.

"I was thinking about my boss, Matt; he's so funny."

"Stop thinking about work," Alicia said playfully.

My hot Alicia, in sunglasses, was in the bucket seat next to me. Her hand reached over. This was the wrong car for doing what she used to do in my Chevy unless she could lean over the center console. I got excited thinking about it.

I put on my sunglasses. I have a problem wearing them for a long time. I wear them briefly, even when driving, regardless of the sun's intensity.

* * *

We had lunch in Tijuana.

In the 1960s, Tijuana's main street, filled with numerous stores and clubs, was only partially paved, leading to dust issues. Water trucks sprayed the unpaved areas to control the dust. Despite its dusty conditions, Tijuana attracted many tourists, primarily from San Diego. Although street food was available, we chose to dine in an air-conditioned restaurant. Inside, I noticed a pair of clean-cut men whom I suspected were from the nearby base. As a former Navy member stationed in San Diego, I knew that visiting Tijuana was against the rules, but many still did so despite the risk of being caught by military police. This was the same reason I found myself in a Tijuana jail for attempting to pay a bar tab with a check. We didn't spend more than ten minutes in TJ after lunch but got back on the highway to Ensenada.

Ensenada is smaller and cleaner than TJ. You have the Pacific Ocean, beaches, and beautiful settings, side by side, with a lack of maintenance and a lack of love for the location. We rented two rooms next to each other with a sliding door from our rooms that opened to the beach. It was marvelous. At twenty dollars a night, the rooms weren't spectacular, but they were okay. The bedding passed Alicia's scrutiny. The minimum wage in the USA was a dollar and fifteen cents per hour, so I guess twenty bucks is not that cheap, but I thought it was. A forty-hour work week was forty-six dollars, and that was before taxes.

It feels like it happened just yesterday. I paid for Clara and Danny's stay, ignoring their protests. The guilt from hurting Danny haunted me, a reminder of how things got out of hand. If I hadn't thrown that punch, it could have been me injured. Yet, the regret stayed with me like a shadow. Settling their hotel bill was a small gesture, my way of trying to make up for the pain he went through during his healing process.

Our agenda for the night was to immerse ourselves in the city's vibrant nightlife, to lose ourselves in the hypnotic beats of the nightclubs. But before we could plunge into that intoxicating chaos, Alicia and I chose to take a slight detour.

We found ourselves drawn to the icy embrace of the Pacific. The Pacific Ocean, with its vast expanse and chilling waters, was a force to be reckoned with. But once you've braved the initial shock, it's a strangely comforting presence.

Without delving into the explicit, let's just say that Alicia and I discovered a new level of intimacy that night. We explored at least five different positions, the cold water of the Pacific serving as our unconventional bed. The sea, with its ever-present glow, was our only witness. It's a peculiar thing, the sea. Even in the darkest of storms, it never truly loses its light.

The thought of sharks lurking beneath us never crossed our minds. We were too engrossed in each other, too consumed by the moment. The thrill, the adrenaline, the sheer exhilaration of it all - it was an experience I wouldn't trade for anything.

* * *

The hotel recommended a nightclub within walking distance. On our way to the club, we passed other businesses. One of them caught our eye. The sign read, Get Married or Divorced, right here, day and night.

We laughed and made our way to the club, a bustling hotspot teeming with energy. Above the bar, a platform served as a stage where women were stripping and dancing, their movements captivating the crowd. Suspended above the stage was a bathtub, adding an intriguing element to the scene. We found a table with a perfect view of both the bar and the main stage.

The atmosphere was electrifying, with dancers gyrating to the pulsating rhythm of rock and roll. Their bodies twirled around two fireman poles, their contagious energy spreading through the room. As we enjoyed our second round of beers, the frothy liquid adding to the heady ambiance, a vision of beauty ascended the stairs leading to the bar stage. The anticipation in the air was palpable, and we couldn't take our eyes off her.

This vision was a young woman of Latin/Mexican descent,

her dark complexion glowing under the stage lights. Her hair, a rich shade of black, cascaded down her back, catching the light and shimmering with each movement. Her eyes were big, round, black eyes sparkled with a mischievous glint, captivating everyone who dared to meet her gaze. There was too much noise to make out what Alicia said, but I felt a pinch on my upper thigh.

As the music played, she began to disrobe, each piece of clothing that fell away revealing more of her tantalizing figure. The crowd erupted into a chorus of whistles and catcalls, the air thick with anticipation. Then, she stood before us in all her glory, her naked form a sight to behold.

She turned the faucets on, and the sound of running water was heard on the speakers, adding to the sensory overload. Something was poured into the tub, and soon, bubbles were visible, adding an element of mystery to the scene. She stepped into the tub, her body disappearing beneath the frothy surface.

The view was somewhat obscured now, with only her upper body visible above the edge of the tub. But then, she raised a leg, or perhaps both, in a provocative manner. The sight of her, partially hidden yet undeniably alluring, sent a wave of erotic energy through the room. The scene was nothing short of intoxicating.

Alicia and Clara whistled loudly. I've never been able to whistle like that. The four of us drank away.

I don't know how many beers later, but I said to Alicia, "You still want to get married?"

Her answer was a long, wet kiss while Clara and Danny applauded. It was too noisy to hear anything but rock and roll blasting.

Danny and Clara were all over each other.

"I want you to be mine," I said to Alicia after the kiss, my lips on her ear.

I'll cut to the chase. All four of us went in to talk to the man in charge of the marriage and divorce place that we passed by on our way to the club from our hotel.

"If the marriage is legal in the country where you get married, it is legal in California," the man in charge explained. He was a little too spiffy to be a preacher, but I guess that's what he was.

Alicia wasn't as drunk as I was at that point, or at least she didn't show it. Me, I was wasted.

"You are saying that if you marry us here, it is legal in Mexico and legal in California," Alicia asked.

"Exactly," he said in good English. I guess his English had to be pretty good if he made a living selling weddings and divorces to drunk tourists. "You want me to marry you? You are a lovely couple."

I looked at Alicia. Maybe we should have waited until tomorrow, but how could I say that when I was the one who brought it up?

Clara spoke before we did.

"We want to get married," she said.

Alicia yelled out in surprise. "Fantastic!"

Danny was beet-red. I hoped he had a job, but he didn't seem unhappy with what was going on. He was smiling a boozy smile and not too steady on his feet.

"Do you have identification, a driver's license?"

The preacher took their information and wrote it down.

"The price is a hundred dollars, cash," he said.

Clara opened her purse and pulled out a hundred-dollar bill just like that.

Alicia put her hand over her mouth and said, "I can't believe this is happening. I had no idea you wanted to get married."

"I didn't know you wanted to marry either," Clara said. "Paul left because you wouldn't marry him."

I thought that was going to start an argument, but Alicia put her arms around me.

"Paul wasn't George," Alicia said.

The preacher walked us into a back room. He turned on the lights, and we saw we were in a chapel. Artificial flowers were all over the place, vases everywhere. A lady in a fancy dress appeared and lit six candles on a candelabra. The chapel looked pretty nice if you didn't look too closely. Someone had gone to a lot of trouble to make a backdrop that would look okay in a picture.

The preacher said to Alicia and me, "Are you the witnesses for this beautiful couple?"

I said, "Of course."

"It would be an honor," Alicia said and hugged Clara for a long time, then hugged Danny. I gave Clara a long hug and shook hands with Danny.

"We have no rings!" Danny said.

"We have rings," the preacher said.

The preacher's helper brought out a display of gold bands.

"They are not real gold," she said. "Ten dollars each."

After a few minutes of trying out rings, Clara and Danny came up with two plain rings. They looked fine to me.

It took the preacher five minutes to marry them and hand them a marriage certificate with a big official-looking stamp. Alicia and I watched the preacher, his assistant, Clara, and Danny as they signed things and accepted the certificate.

"What happened to us?" Alicia whispered and turned to me with a sad expression.

I put one hand on each side of her face. "Are you sure you want to do this?"

"I'm certain," she sighed. "Don't you? Don't you love me enough?"

I was intoxicated but not completely drunk, or else I wouldn't recall it now after decades. I should have been influenced by the negative experience I had with Selena, my first marriage. It was me who was eager to get married back then, and now I found myself facing Alicia, who was also eager.

Thirty minutes later, the four of us exited with the documents that declared us as husband and wife. Our ladies had delicate flower crowns adorning their heads, and each held a small bouquet adorned with colorful ribbons. As we stepped onto the sidewalk, our ladies let out loud whistles. Danny embraced Clara, and I embraced Alicia. Passing cars honked their horns, and some people leaned out of their car windows, whistling in celebration.

Alicia and I had already been intimately involved in every way for a year. Our desire for each other still burned strong. We returned to our hotel and attempted to continue our passion in the shower, but the space was too cramped. Instead, we opened the doors facing the sea and joined each other on the bed. The sound of the crashing waves served as an arousing backdrop to our intimate encounter. If I were a coyote, I would have howled with pleasure.

* * *

I'll skip the part about how my mom took the news of my getting married to Alicia, whom she had never met. My dad was a trooper and welcomed Alicia with open arms. My mom had her reservations but hugged her.

"We can live in the apartment," Alicia suggested. "Danny and Clara in their bedroom; we are in ours. We can split the rent until you are set so we can move."

"I don't want to live with another couple," I said. "Let's move into my parents' basement. It's almost finished. The bathroom is new, and there's no kitchen, but we're not going to be there long. Or we can move into my bedroom. You saw it. It's bigger than your bedroom."

I still called it a basement because that's what it used to be before the walls were covered with drywall, the electrical work was done, and the plumbing for the bathroom. If we were to stay there, all we needed was a stove and a hood. A kitchen sink was already there in a nice cabinet.

"Your mom doesn't like me," Alicia said with a tell-me-I'm-wrong chuckle.

"My mom is like that," I said. "It will take her a while to warm up."

"I'll go crazy in the basement while you're at work," she said.

"My sister Mary has a sitter who is there during the day. My parents are at work all day."

Alicia had one condition.

"I'm not giving up my bedroom. I couldn't possibly bring all my clothes to your parents' house."

After Alicia moved in, the first day when I got home from work, she was upstairs in the living room playing with my sister, Mary.

I offered to take her out to dinner, but she said my mom had dinner prepared. My mom worked like crazy and still came home to cook. Leonard helped her a lot. He got home before my mom and started whatever dinner was supposed to be.

Our second night in the basement went okay. The bed was new. There were plenty of windows with good views of downtown Los Angeles. It wasn't a dungeon. The ceilings were taller than eight feet because the house was built into the hill. The television from my bedroom had started off in the den until it got replaced, and it went from my bedroom to our place downstairs. Two stuffed chairs that had also started off in the living room moved from my bedroom to our place downstairs, though we only needed one.

"Fuck look at the view," Alicia said.

We sat in the backyard, which had the same view that the balcony above us had. Nothing was blocking our direct shot to downtown Los Angeles. The building that stood out the most was City Hall.

Sometimes Alicia and I went out to dinner. A few days after we started staying at my parents, we saw Danny and Clara. I received a kiss from Clara that I thought would surely anger Danny, but he was cool. His jaw had healed okay with no scars, and he had a pleasant smile. I learned that he worked as a forklift operator at Certified Grocers, a significant grocery outlet in East

Los Angeles. He was in a union and seemed to earn a good income.

"As long as Alicia has her things here and her bedroom is still hers, I'll pay half the rent as she's been doing," I told Danny.

Danny liked that. Clara already knew. She did not plan to quit her job at Bullock's Department Store.

"I may start looking for a job," Alicia said, looking from Clara to me.

"You never have to work," I said, "but I'm not going to stop you if that's what you want to do."

I got a kiss for that.

* * *

Alicia went out to apply for jobs downtown. When I got home, we went out to dinner.

We sat across from each other in a booth at the restaurant in Chinatown. A waiter brought us menus.

"Your mom is so cute," Alicia said, looking over the menu. "When I told her that we were passing on dinner, she said, 'It's your loss.'"

I laughed.

"Did she say it in English or Spanish?"

"In English. Her English is getting good."

"You haven't known her but a few days," I said. "How would you know?"

"I don't know how she was before, just what I hear now. Hey, I'm trying to be nice."

We ordered. The waiter was an older man with not very good English. He brought us a couple of little pots of Chinese tea and poured us cups full. Alicia stirred in a boatload of sugar.

The soup came. I passed on the soup here but munched the

crunchies. Alicia spooned her hot and sour soup and pushed her little bowl of fried wontons in my direction.

When the main dishes came out soon after, Alicia asked for chopsticks. She wasn't very good at using them, and her laughter at her clumsiness with chopsticks kept interrupting the story she told me about the jobs she had applied for downtown. She'd put in an application at Bullocks where Clara worked.

"I can support us," I said, knowing I could. I just needed a few more paychecks to give us a cushion.

"I know you can support us. I need to go back to work to speed up getting out of the basement."

I simply nodded. "You're right. I'll make that a priority," I assured her. As I spoke, memories of the cramped back rooms where Selena and I resided flooded my mind. I had grown accustomed to our meager existence, mistakenly thinking it was acceptable. Perhaps Selena despised our living conditions but kept her true feelings concealed.

"Do you hate living where we're living?" Words just slipped out.

"I don't want to pressure you."

"Tell me, do you hate it?"

Alicia smiled. She stopped eating and looked at me with her big beautiful eyes. "I hate it. It would be so cool if we were staying in my room at Clara's." Before I could say anything. "Baby, let's eat, going to get cold."

We ate without a word about the basement. Alicia brought up a new topic.

"Did I ever tell you that Clara started working at Bullock's because she thought a talent scout might discover her someday?"

"No, I didn't know."

When she got hired at Bullock's, they gave her a choice of Beverly Hills or Downtown. She didn't want to make the long drive and chose Downtown. Since then, she has always mentioned that it was a poor decision. The talent scouts who frequent department stores are likely in Beverly Hills.

"Yeah, Bullocks is a fancy store. When I was younger, I used to go in there."

Alicia chased a piece of lemon chicken around the plate and finally speared it like the chopstick was a fork. She ate it in two bites and put down the chopstick. She looked at me a little skeptically.

"You must have been really young. You joined the Navy, got married, ended up in the brig, got drummed out of the Navy, and then spent all that time in Youth Authority. Are you sure you're twenty?"

"Correction, prison. I don't consider DVI Youth Authority."

"Okay, prison? You should stop calling it that. It sounds bad."

"When I'm over it, I will." I sighed.

"So did your mother take you to Bullocks when you were a kid?"

"No, it was all about one of my first jobs. Want to hear?"

"Always, baby."

I told her about the summer when I worked for the women's clothes distributor in [1]Leonard's building. I shared how the shipping guy, employed there, would push racks of clothes along the sidewalk to major stores like Bullocks, which purchased the clothes from the distributor where I worked.

"If you were delivering dresses and things to Bullocks, they had to be expensive stuff."

"I didn't know much about pricing back then, but all the garments were prettier than anything my mom had in her closet."

Alicia listened intently to my words, then bestowed upon me

---

1. Leonard was my step-dad

one of those tender, affectionate smiles. Deep down, I kept to myself the realization of the age difference between us. The four-year gap she had over me mirrored the gap between Selena and me. At times, their smiles seemed almost maternal, exuding a sense of approval. It may sound absurd, but that's how it made me feel.

* * *

The next day, I called Leonard to see what he wanted from Bob's Hamburgers, but he opted out. I brought home take-out for Alicia and me, and Leonard heated Mom's dinner.

Alicia and I didn't have a dining room table, so when I bought the bed and mattress, I also got a card table and four folding chairs. We had space in what would be the kitchen someday. Nothing was wrong with our appetites, and we polished off our messy hamburgers and chili fries.

"I promise we won't be here long," I said to Alicia.

She flashed one of those endearing smiles in between bites of her food.

* * *

That night, we lay on the bed facing each other in the dark. The windows were open, and we were enjoying the breeze.

"Maybe your parents can loan you some money. We could rent a place and move right away."

"They don't have any money like that. I already promised we'd get out of here fast." I heard a sigh. "Okay, baby."

"Thank you," I murmured softly, the words just a breath escaping my lips. Leaning in, I tenderly pressed my lips against hers, savoring the warmth and familiarity of her touch. Alicia's response to physical contact was always profound, a gentle spark igniting in her eyes as my hand brushed against her breast. Despite the late hour shrouding the world outside in serene quietness, we yielded to the moment.

Our movements were hesitant, as if lost in our own contemplations. This time, it was fleeting, overshadowed by my preoccupation with her discontent about where we lived. She hated the basement.

Amidst the post-climax quiet, with her head nestled on my chest, I sensed the tension in her frame. She was really uptight. Sleep found us.

I used to start my day with a refreshing morning shower, gearing up to conquer the challenges ahead. The evening shower awaited me at home, symbolizing the act of washing away the day's burdens. Fatigue never betrayed me, for a shower held the cure, but Matt's demands pushed me to my limits. Today the mere memory of those intense days exhausts me.

Upon returning home, I bypassed the usual spaces and headed straight for the basement, assuming Alicia was upstairs with my parents. Post-shower, as I dressed, Alicia's absence lingered. A quick check upstairs revealed Leonard and my mother enjoying dinner, unaware of Alicia's whereabouts.

Alicia and I were married for twenty-four days.

I could have questioned how easily we were walking away from the marriage deal, but I didn't say anything.

Twenty-four days after we were married, we went in separate cars to the scene of our vows to dissolve them. I drove alone to the preacher's place in Ensenada. Alicia had her own car. Her ex-boyfriend, Paul, whom I had never seen or met before, drove her to ax our marriage. In this second marriage, like the first one, there was another man.

I could write chapters about how it came to this. I figure the bottom line is what's important. The bottom line is that we got divorced.

Chapter 7
Weekend

Nine hours after I left my parents' house for Ensenada, I was back. I hurt, but I wasn't torn like I had been in Juarez. Maybe I was getting used to short-term marriages.

"Maybe it's for the best, son," my mother said right off.

Leonard didn't say anything. I think he was studying me to get a feel of how I was taking it.

The next morning, I was off to work. Matt and I were getting more talkative while working, but the conversation stopped on a dime if Matt thought it was distracting me.

We were on another Thrifty roof. Sparks flew. I had my goggles on and was welding a coupling joining two four-inch diameter, twenty-foot copper pipes. It's really soldering, but back then we used silver floss, and you had to heat the metal nearly as hot as you do for welding metal to metal.

"Matt, I got divorced this weekend."

"What? That's two down, boy. What the fuck?"

"Shit happens," I said.

He moved over close. Even with the goggles on, I could see his face from the corner of my eye.

"You're getting good with the torch," he said.

"Thanks."

"Next time just live together. Why run out and get married?"

"It's easy to get married. Easy to get divorced. We were out in twenty minutes with a divorce certificate."

His chuckle was too quiet for me to hear over the torch.

"I been married thirty-five years to my Lucy. Wouldn't think of divorcing her."

I looked up at him through my dark goggles and held the torch away from the pipe.

"God bless your marriage for another hundred years."

He walked away, but I know he liked what I said.

I was eating a plate of Chinese takeout on the card table with the TV on when the phone rang. I turned off the TV, walked over to the window, opened it, and sat down on the bed. I clicked off the light and felt the cool breeze on my bare chest. I'd already had a shower. I could eat later.

"I heard what happened," Clara said on the phone. "I'm sorry."

"Thanks," I said. "Is she living there?"

"She hasn't said anything about moving out, but she's at Paul's house."

"Tell me the truth. Are they a thing?" I asked. "Did she ever get over him?"

"Soon as he dropped the marriage requirement, they were hooked up again. That is between us," she said.

"I'm not surprised. It's the same thing that happened with Selena."

"Are you okay?" Clara asked, sounding compassionate.

"I'm okay," I said. "I'm telling everybody I'm getting used to short term marriages."

"You sound okay."

"I'm good. Going to miss you," I said.

"I am here any time you want to talk."

I wanted to tell her I'd miss the threesome. I wanted to tell her I really liked doing it with her when we did it.

"I think about you a lot," she said.

"Really?"

"I do," she said.

"What about Danny?"

"What about him?" she said.

"I like you Clara, always have. I'm jealous of Danny. He's got a fox."

"If you ever want to meet up, let me know," she said suggestively. It was the way she said that which turned me on.

If I took her up on it, I'd be doing the same thing that Sergio had done with my wife. Danny is not my pal, just as I wasn't Sergio's pal when he met up with her. I didn't need to go looking for a fight when Danny found out I was sneaking off with his wife. There were plenty of women who were not married.

The ride with Alicia and Clara was wild and exciting. For me, it was worth a year-plus of my life. No regrets.

* * *

I filled out an application to rent a fantastic two-bedroom apartment on College View Drive in Monterey Park, a pristine area with brand new houses and apartments above Atlantic Boulevard only a short distance from a terrible part of East Los

Angeles. There were fourteen units, a big swimming pool, a sauna bath, and a small gym. The rent was a hundred twenty dollars with a two-hundred-dollar deposit. The apartment came furnished.

I showed the manager my bank account with over two thousand dollars in it, I didn't list the bonuses that Matt gave me, but I wrote that I was in the Union working for WESPAC and how much I made. The manager approved me on the spot. The rental agreement I signed required a thirty-day notice if I wanted to move.

Some years later, I bought the apartment building and made my mom an offsite manager. I bought several properties on that street and single homes above in the hills. I leased out the homes, and the rental income paid the mortgages. More later.

Chapter 8
Independence, ELA

While I was moving into the apartment building, I saw a pretty brunette just getting out of the pool. Her body was smoking. My hands were full of clothes on hangers. I almost walked past her but stopped to introduce myself.

"My name is George. Do you live here?"

She stepped off the pool's ladder and squeezed water out of her hair.

"I do," she said, looking at the clothes I was carrying. "Aren't those heavy?"

"You should see what I carry at work," I said.

"Let me help you."

She picked up what I had in my left hand. "I'm Ava," she said. "Where are we going? What's your apartment?"

I was right in front of the pool, apartment two. Like a dummy, I had not parked in my spot and had to carry my clothes through the front entry, and then along the pool to my apartment. I wouldn't have met Ava as fast as I did if I had parked in the right place and come up the back stairs to my place. All the first-level apartments have a back exit to parking. Ava brought this to my attention.

"I live right next door," she said as we walked.

She came in behind me, and after the clothes were hung, I extended my hand.

"What kind of greeting is that?" she asked. She hugged me, and my shirt went soggy.

"I'm not thinking," Ava said. "I'm getting your carpet all wet. I'm sorry."

She double-timed it out the door for her towel that was laid out on a pool recliner.

Ava shared an apartment with Emma, a delightful person with red hair that I'm not particularly fond of. Although it suited Emma, I have a personal aversion to red hair. In contrast, Ava was a perfect ten out of ten in my eyes.

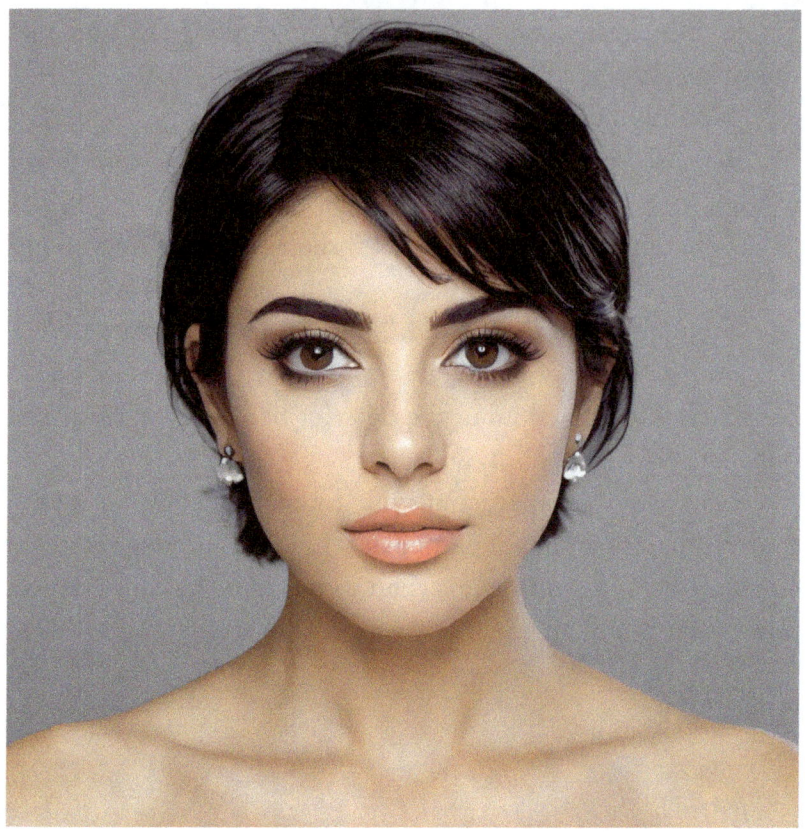

Ava

* * *

I had to make three trips from my mom's house. Ava was so friendly that I couldn't get over it. She insisted on helping me. She rode with me to my mother's house and helped me pack my stuff in the back seat and trunk. It took a lot of trips from the house to the car. Impalas carry more than you'd think.

"God, did you hold up a department store or something?" Ava asked.

I wanted to say, 'Yes, in fact, I did.' I wanted to say that it was a locker thing. I just laughed like she'd made a joke.

Emma came along on the last trip. The Impala had bucket seats, so Emma sat in the back.

Emma

"If we fill the back, I'll squeeze in with Ava," Emma said. "Don't worry about it."

There was no way I would end up in a relationship with these two foxes like I'd had with Alicia and Clara, but I felt comfortable with them already.

"I can't get over how hot the two of you are," I said, with my eyes on the road. Mostly.

They laughed.

"How old are you?"

"Twenty. Almost legal."

"I got you beat by three years, Georgie," Emma said.

"I just turned legal two months ago," Ava said and touched my ear. I got all chilled.

"You got nothing to worry about, Georgie. I'll buy beer when you want," Emma said.

"Dig that," I said.

"Hey, I'm legal, too," Ava said.

When we were done, and back at my apartment, I carried in my shoes in pillowcases. I didn't know where to put them.

"Seriously, where did you get all these clothes?" Ava asked.

"I didn't steal them," I lied.

I had a little mental dialogue with myself. 'Actually, I didn't take them out of the store. That would be stealing.' The other side of my head said, 'You did steal them.'

I shrugged. "I like shoes," I said.

Ava and Emma's apartment was on the same level, next door.

It's pretty cool when you're twenty, have a good job, a new car, and spending money.

"Hungry?" I asked.

They were. I would have taken them anywhere. I drove them to Shakey's Pizza on Atlantic—their choice.

"I can't get over these wheels," Emma said.

"I get all wet and horny," Ava said, "The new car smell."

I refrained from telling them that the car had already been christened. That would have been stupid.

After the pizza, we returned to their apartment because mine had not been put together yet. I had nothing in the refrigerator. I stopped at a liquor store and gave Emma twenty dollars to buy beer. Ava and I waited in the car.

Their living room was practically identical to mine. All the units were furnished. I sat in an upholstered armchair. They got on the sofa.

"Break my heart and tell me if you have boyfriends or are married."

"I see men, but I have no relationship," Ava said.

"Same here," Emma said. "How about you?'

"I just got a divorce. My marriage lasted twenty-four days."

"Oh no," Ava said.

"I'm fine," I said. That was all about me I was going to tell them. I broke that thread by asking what they did for a living.

"We both work," Emma said. She had nice teeth. Up close like this, her red hair didn't bother me at all, or maybe it was the thing beer does improving vision. At least I didn't have work tomorrow, and I didn't have to drive home.

Bitchin.

"I work construction," I said.

It was easier just to say construction than to explain the air-conditioning thing. Most people got confused and started asking questions.

"You must make good money to own that car and have all the clothes," Ava said, taking a swig from her Budweiser.

"I do okay," I said. "How about you two?"

"We do okay," Emma said. "We're escorts."

At twenty, I was not sure what an escort was.

"What kind of escort?" I asked.

"You got to be kidding," Ava said.

"You don't have to tell me," I said.

Emma got up from the sofa and came over to the chair where I was. A second later, she was on my lap, hands holding my face as she moved close. She giggled softly and whispered, "We have sex for pay."

Ava was on the sofa smiling steadily and watching us.

In the Navy, we didn't call girls who did this escorts. Juarez was filled with prostitutes. I remembered the sex for pay I had in San Diego while on leave from boot camp. It was the first and only time I paid for sex.

I had another beer.

They matched me a beer for beer. They could drink.

"How do you drink beer and keep the luscious bodies you have? I almost dropped the clothes I was carrying when I saw you, Ava. I was awestruck."

They didn't explain how they kept their figures. I wanted to ask how they got their customers if they made good money, and what they charged. I had paid fifty dollars in San Diego, the first time I paid for sex.

These two ladies were like dreams walking. They must have had a bunch of men hot for them.

My curiosity got the better of me.

"How do you get your customers?"

"We pay a guy to handle it. We don't have to go out in the street," Ava said.

Live and learn. When I asked her if she lived here, it never for a moment occurred to me that she was a rent-me girl. She was too good for that type of work, young and perfect-looking and, except for the red hair, Emma too.

"I see," I said.

"You are a stone's throw away," Emma said. "Don't hesitate to ask if you need anything."

"You won't hesitate, will you?" Ava asked.

She gave me their phone number.

I kissed Ava. I was going to ask how much for kissing. Fortunately, I managed to hold my tongue.

Around midnight, I thanked them for helping me move and for the company and kissed them goodnight. I wondered if I had taken them away from business and if I should give them money. I didn't have sex with them.

***

I was asleep on Sunday morning when the phone guy showed up at eight.

"I didn't think you guys worked today."

"I can reschedule you," he said.

"No way. Come in. Go for it."

"I'm installing two phones, one in the bedroom and one where?"

"In the living room at this jack. Let me show you the jack in the bedroom."

After I showered, I pulled out my old phone book that had turned up in the course of my move. A cool guy might call it a black book, but it's too humble for that, a tiny battered thing, ragged from living in my pocket and being dragged through the Navy, Juarez, Tijuana, the brig, DVI, and in and out of my parent's house. It had made the cut to my new digs. For the first time, I had my own phone line. I was inspired to open it up. It housed old numbers that were no longer in use like Thelma and Patty's.

I made a call that I had never thought that I would make.

I called Luna at her parents' house.

"Bueno. Ramirez residence," the housekeeper answered.

"Luna, por favor," I said.

"Luna no vive aquí. Quiere su numero?" [1]

She was probably married by now. It was an American phone number. I added Luna's name to the book - and wrote the number down, and continued doing things to get the house in order. I drove to Ralph's Market and picked out basic necessities. I did not plan to cook, but I needed cheese, cold cuts, crackers

---

1. Luna doesn't live here. Do you want her phone number?

and bread for lunch, munchies, beer, fruit, things a bachelor keeps in the kitchen.

I didn't drink alone, but I'd never had my own apartment before. I opened a beer and sat down in the den by my new phone and old phone book. The call I made was inevitable.

"Alo?"

"Luna, it's me. Hang up if you got a husband."

There were peals of laughter on her end.

"Kenito, I cannot believe this. It must be because I went to mass this morning."

"So, you aren't married?"

"No, I'm not married. I'm in El Paso at the university. I have my own apartment."

"It's good to hear your voice."

"How are you? Why did you wait so long to call?"

"When you stopped writing me back I figured I stop bothering you."

"You never bothered me!"

"Again, thanks for driving my car all the way to Los Angeles."

"I would do more than that for you, Kenito."

"You the best," I said.

Laughter. "You only tried me once, and that was in the car. Is that what you mean?"

"You're so funny, Luna."

"Kenito, I have a class, and I'm running late. Call me later."

"I'll call you," I said and hung up. "Your English is great!"

She had hung up.

The call ended abruptly, and I can't quite recall what was going through my mind at the time, but I never called Luna back. I never saw her again. I suspect she must have been lying about having a class since it was Sunday. It felt like a deliberate brush-off, and I realized she wanted me to understand that.

After I finished my first beer, I opened the front window blinds, looking out at the pool. Ava and Emma had the same view.

If Ava and Emma hosted their customers at home, I bet they would have come up the back stairs. It was more private that way, so it was a perfect setup.

I could just run over there, but what if they were busy? She could have given me the phone number so I would call rather than come over.

I dialed the number and got a voice.

"Hi, this is your neighbor; call me." I hung up.

Damn, I didn't leave my number. I didn't have a phone last night and didn't have a number to give them. Fuck.

I had been looking for a one-bedroom, but they only had this apartment available, and the rent was twenty dollars more than a one-bedroom. I was glad I'd gotten it. Two bedrooms. Two closets. I spent two hours putting away what needed putting away, including almost all my shoes.

The front door was right next to the window. I saw Ava through the window before she knocked, and I sprang out of my chair.

"Hey, good afternoon," I said.

She kissed my cheek. She was in short shorts with a shirttail wrapped above her belly button. She wore sandals. She smelled like she'd just gotten out of the shower.

"Back at you," she said, walking in.

"I see a beer can; you must have gone to the store. How did you get it?"

"I bought a case along with my groceries, and the clerk said nothing."

"Sweet."

"I'll get you one."

"Nah, I have company in thirty minutes. You seem stressed," Ava said.

"It's getting used to the apartment," I said. "Hey, I got a phone now. I called you."

"When you call, do what you did today, either say hi or neighbor, no phone."

"Got it."

"It was a nice visit last night," she said, sitting on my sofa.

"I felt right at home at your place. Many thanks for that."

"You said you got divorced. Anyone taking care of your sex needs?"

I sat in an easy chair beside her. What I didn't ask the night before, I did now. "How much?"

Ava laughed but didn't blush.

"We're neighbors, and we dig you. If we're free and available, we're free and available. Don't sweat how much."

"You have rent and expenses. Tell me how much."

I had no clue what pussy went for. Was it fifty like the time in San Diego?

"Our regular customers that don't come through the pimp pay between twenty to forty dollars. They get off and split."

"Is that good money?"

"Money is good as long as we have the customers."

"Of course," I said.

Ava looked at her watch and got up. "I got to run."

"What's Emma doing? Is she busy?"

"She should be finishing up in a few. She can take a shower and come over. Whatever your stress, she'll suck it right out of you."

I thought of Alicia and had to laugh.

"Only if I can pay her," I said.

"Give her a ten, and she'll be happy."

"I'll be here," I said. I walked her to the door, opened it, and she kissed me before stepping out.

I was making eight bucks an hour plus hefty bonuses from Matt. A ten wasn't bad to get sex with no strings. Fuck. Good deal. Even if I paid twenty dollars.

* * *

The union rules were for all members. Matt and I were sitting on folding canvas stools I'd bought to use on days we didn't eat in his truck or take a five-minute break. We were having lunch on the roof of a job. Matt had been a loyal union member for decades, but he didn't always follow the break rules. I was okay with that. I was soaking up so much experience and receiving bonuses when we finished a job. In almost every job we'd completed so far, Matt received a bonus, and he would share a portion with me. I never inquired about the exact amount he received. Nevertheless, he never gave me less than three hundred. I worked all week to earn just a little more than that.

I'd been bringing my lunch in a paper bag, most often from some fast-food joint where I'd purchased it. Now my own refrigerator had cold cuts, and my kitchen had bread. I was still working out this lunch thing, now that I had my own place. Matt's lunch was in a metal lunch box, thermos brand, the old classic one that looked like a top-opening mailbox. He usually carried a couple of sandwiches wrapped in wax paper, a piece of fruit, and some leftover dessert from home like a chunk of cake. There was always his massive thermos, usually full of coffee. In the winter, sometimes there was soup. I think his wife packed his lunch, but that's not something I asked him about.

"Did you do anything else before this? The department store, drugstore, paperboy?"

"Let's see. One thing leads to the next. Before cashiering at the drugstore, I delivered for them. That happened because, during one spring break, I was a courier for Red Arrow Messenger Service. Technically, I worked for United Parcel which owns Red Arrow, but we Red Arrow employees rode bikes. After that, I worked in shipping for a fashion distributor. That led to the drugstore. This was all in Los Angeles."

"That's a lot of work history for someone your age. You never stop amazing me, kid."

I didn't bring up the Navy.

Matt grunted a little, a good grunt. He polished off the sandwich he'd been eating and pulled out another one.

"My wife and I are going to Paris. The first time we have been away that far."

"Wow, Paris, good for you, Matt."

"I'm asking management to put you with Henry while I'm gone. Henry works startup. You are not ready to do startup on the apprentice program, but you'll get the flavor of it during the three weeks I'm gone."

I don't recall exactly when it started, but at this point, I drove to Matt's house in the morning, left my car parked on the street, and rode with him in his old truck when the job we were working on was farther than fifty miles from city hall. He always drove. Sometimes we talked during the drive and sometimes not. He only turned on the radio to hear KNX news.

Once, while he was waiting for lunch, he invited me in and introduced me to his wife. His house was a nice two story in the Los Felix area where there are some big homes. The family car parked on the driveway was a Buick, newish but not new. It made me think. After five years of apprenticeship, I would become a journeyman. The pay scale was damn good. Matt may have money in the bank, but his house was not special, his truck had seen better days, the Buick could be newer, and well-it's a Buick.

I was with my mom when she operated her own flower shop and the same with my dad with his numerous businesses and the curio store, he'd had in Agua Prieta. For better or for worse, my parents had been in business for themselves. For the most part, I loved my job, but the short time I'd had the ice cream parlor made me feel like I had the makings of being more than just an employee. I want new everything and to live in a big house. My negative moments didn't stop me from sucking up everything Matt taught me.

In the early morning, Henry had me drive to West Covina, park my car, and he would drive us both to the site, the first job being an auditorium at a university in Thousand Oaks, a long drive from West Covina. This guy had a van filled with technical equipment. Everything about startup is pretty clean work.

The neighborhood where he lived was more upscale, and Henry's house looked bigger than Matt's. There were three new cars parked outside his house every morning I came by. Still, I was looking to do more. I had no clue what kind of business I would start if I had an opportunity again. I forced myself to stay on track with the job I had. Maybe one day, I could own my own WESPAC like my employer. Why not? The dream of having my own business was not gone, just set aside until opportunity knocked.

Henry was the most patient person I had ever met. He went out of his way to explain each instrument we used. Once he saw that I could handle a ladder-how could I not after working with Matt? -Henry had me taking airflow readings from each register in the auditorium. Some of these were nosebleed high. Someone afraid of heights would not do what I did. I tagged each register with wall-safe tape and wrote the number and reading that I was getting from the instrument on a strap around my neck. After you go up and down a ladder fifty times with that thing around your neck, you feel it.

"George, take a break," Henry said. "We don't rush startup like Matt does his end."

"Got it. Thanks."

I kept a log. Henry expected it to be extremely legible and reflect each reading. The airflow was neither hot nor cold. The big compressors that I had helped hook up had not been started up yet. They had not yet been filled with Freon gas from the big tanks.

By my third week, we were still on the auditorium job, but now we were charging the compressors with gas using the same gauges I had used in DVI to fill the small refrigerator compressor. We were now using big monster machines. The principal was the same, and all tied in with what I was learning at LA Trade Tech class I took every other week.

Matt returned from his trip. I went back to work with him on a new construction, a five-story office building in Van Nuys, California. When we needed the equipment located on the roof, Matt coordinated with the general contractor. Matt measured. I spray-canned lines, tagging what went where. Not all jobs did this crane stuff at night, but the loading would take place at night.

"I can come at night," I offered.

"These fools will get it right or else," Matt said.

With all the markings we had put on the rooftop, they'd have to be blind not to get it right.

There were nights when I reminisced about hitting the clubs like Christine and I used to do. Back then, I was so young, and the biggest thrill was the sheer audacity of it all. It should be easier now, even though I still hadn't reached that magic age. I made friends easily, but none of them were truly close. My time in prison had taken me out of the social scene, and even before that, I was always wrapped up in a long-term relationship. I yearned to break free. I needed someone—not a wife or a girlfriend, just someone to share moments with.

Ava and Emma, well, I got sex for pay and dug it. I didn't have to use what Christine taught me about satisfying my partner, but I did that. It is part of the fun. I dug that there were no strings. No need to talk about love. No talk about shortchanging the cash register like with Christine. No apologies to Patty for not paying her mom. No conversation about the locker thing.

I hadn't seen my neighbors at the same time since the night we had beer at their apartment. I didn't try to figure out who I liked more, Ava or Emma. Emma was a keg of dynamite. Ava was more serious. If she was on top, she'd ask if it was okay and would offer to do another position. Ava was not a novice, but I'd say Emma had more experience. She was the older one. Positively ancient, all of twenty-two.

When I paid them, they both played at being hesitant to take it. Maybe they were serious and really didn't want to charge me. Now that I knew sex was their business, I could not take it free like a mooch.

Growing up, I was an organized, clean kid. I knew how to wash and iron, so my clothes and my person were always clean. I couldn't go a day without showering, way back when my mom and dad gave me a choice to shower in the morning or night. In boot camp, I was brainwashed as were the other sailors about hygiene and orderly everything. With that said, Ava and Emma were squeaky clean.

* * *

The oil massage that Patty used to give me was my introduction to massage, and it was something I missed. Ava gave me a solution and hooked me up with a girl named Cathy, who did massage house calls. Cathy was older than me, but so was everyone. She was under thirty, and when I asked her how she got her biceps so toned, she told me she lifted weights.

"Lightweights," she said. "Want to check out my abs?"

I thought that Cathy might be in the same business as Ava and Emma, but she wasn't. She was a health freak, and she didn't mind taking her clothes off or keeping them on. I chose nude.

I was okay with my body but not at my peak. The Navy had pushed me to my max, and I'd fooled around with weights at DVI, but nothing since I was home. I still had sixteen-inch biceps but nothing going in the abs department. If I didn't start lifting and curling, I was in danger of losing what took so long to build. I thought about using the second bedroom as some sort of gym, but the room was furnished as a bedroom. Cathy didn't seem to care one way or another.

"You can't touch," she said. She had a super fine body.

The massage was on a bed like when Patty massaged me. Cathy brought a sheet to put over the bed because she used oil. I'm not sure what she had at her house for massage, but I don't remember seeing anything that looked like a massage table back then. During the day, Cathy worked at a chiropractic office as a therapist. She was not a chiropractor.

"Nine out of ten massages, I do at my house," she said. "I also work weekends. I can go for an hour or longer."

When she turned me face up, I was hard as a bat. She massaged around me and didn't touch it. I may have been left sex thirsty, but my body was feeling great. I gave her ten dollars[2] and that included a tip.

Try and get a massage house call in 2020 for ten dollars.

I had a towel around me when I walked her to the door at eight in the evening.

---

2. Adjusted for inflation, $10.00 in 1963 is equal to $84.53 in 2020.

"By the way," she said, "I'm having a party for my niece. She graduated from cosmetology school. Want to come?"

"I'd love to," I said. "I won't know anyone there."

"It's okay. It's a friendly crowd. Maybe you and my niece will take to each other."

"Nice," I said. "Give me the details."

She handed me a sealed envelope.

"Here is an invite with the address and phone. Don't bring a gift."

"Cathy, thanks for the invite and for the massage."

"Call me again," she said, "I can use the business."

"Count on it."

I had to work the next day. I called Ava and held my breath, hoping I got one of them and not the answering machine.

"Can you talk?"

"Talk to me, G."

"Your friend Cathy just left. Great hands. Fine job she did, but I'm stiff as a board."

"I'll be right over."

* * *

"Cathy is straight as an arrow," Ava said. "Her hands are sweet."

"I loved the massage," I said. One look at Ava's perfect legs and ass, and I was hard again in a split second.

"G, come on, let's take care of that. Want it here or bedroom."

I lay down on the unmade bed. She got on top and wham, I was inside. I stopped. I raised up on my elbows to better see her sitting on me.

"What?" Her eyes wide.

"I don't want to be rushed," I said. "You sure you got time?"

"G, I never rushed you. I got time."

Two hours later, when Ava got dressed to leave, she said, "I'm going home to bed. I can't handle a gig tonight. You wore me out."

"Wait," I said. I jumped out of bed naked, reached for my jeans pocket, and came up with forty dollars.

"This time, it was from the heart," she said. "Put the money back in your pocket."

"That's cool, in that case, it's a gift. Take the money, please."

She looked at the two twenties and took one. "I'm good with this."

I kissed her.

I hugged her. She hugged me. Wet Kisses.

By her own words, Ava was an escort, but she was a young woman with feelings.

"I love the way you fuck me," she said. "I never come with tricks."

We landed back on the bed.

Ava

"Stay the night, and you can keep calling me G."

"Only if you hug me. I want to be hugged all night."

"Deal," I said. "I love hugging you."

I watched her undress. It only took a second. Before we passed out, we did it all over again. I don't know how much later it was that the doorbell rang. A knock on the front door woke up Ava and me. It was way after midnight.

It sounded urgent, so I rushed through the living room, putting on my jeans and walking. Might have gotten there a little faster if I'd sat down to do it, or at least stood still. I nearly took out the lamp and the end table but managed to right myself and my unbroken lamp and opened the front door with only my jeans on.

It was Emma, with her hair messed up, her face flushed, makeup melting, mascara giving her raccoon eyes. Her cheek was red, like she'd been slapped.

"Is Ava here?"

"What's wrong?" I pulled her into the house and shut the door.

Ava came to the living room, buttoning up, her shirt, her shorts, and sandals already on.

"I'll handle Jaimie," she said.

In the light of the lamp, I examined Emma's cheek. She'd been slapped, maybe punched too. A well-defined red imprint of a hand stained her cheek.

"Who did this to you?" I clenched my fist.

Ava put her arm around Emma. "We'll be fine, G. Go back to bed, please. Don't come out. Jaime is where our business comes from."

"I'm going to be standing here until you tell me all is okay," I said.

"He knows better than to mess up our looks," Ava said.

"It's true, G. Don't worry. This was just a slap," Emma said, like it was nothing like she wasn't hiccoughing away the remains of her tears, and her eyes red from crying.

I was red with fury to think a guy hit a woman. It was like in movies I hated to see, or in the old neighborhood where domestic squabbles were a way of life.

The girls stepped out and closed the door.

I didn't hear any yelling and my living room wall is on the other side of their apartment. Too many tenants were around, and the manager's apartment was across the pool. It was quiet. In a way, I thought it was smart of them not to make a fuss if they were keeping their business a secret. But the silence was worrisome. I had to find out what it meant.

I dialed their apartment. Ava answered.

"He's gone. He was pissed because I wasn't available for work. I'm sorry you had to see that G."

"Sorry for what? Did he hit you too?"

"He didn't. He's gone. You got to work in a few hours. Go back to bed, G."

"Thanks for the wonderful time," I said.

"It gets better, G. I like you."

In the background, Emma said, "Tell him so do I."

I turned off the light and crashed till it was time to get up, at least technically. I tossed and turned.

* * *

At six in the morning, I was out of the shower and in my car fifteen minutes later. I went to my assigned space, where my car was parked next to a fire extinguisher on the wall. I turned the ignition, and a guy knocked on my car window. I hadn't noticed him, but he must have been waiting for me.

I didn't know him but had run across plenty of younger versions of him at DVI. Sure, I was generalizing, but I read the way he was posturing, like a pissed-off junkyard dog. The chip on his shoulder was massive. This guy was about forty, seriously good-looking, probably Puerto Rican. His nose was perfect, his cheekbones and chin perfect, like he'd gotten his face from some actor. He had a lot of gold around his neck, and the hairy finger he was using to poke my car window wore a large ring. He was wearing the standard jeans and t-uniform, and the heavy gold chain around his neck didn't look right on him.

"Step away from my car," I said, staring at his mug. He had a heavy brow ridge with an excess of eyebrows. Needed a shave. No gray in his five o'clock shadow.

"You want to fuck Ava? You pay me. Understand motherfucker?"

My window was still closed. He gave it a couple of thumps with his knuckles.

This was the guy who had hit Emma. A woman I liked. I knew the type. I hate bullies who slap around people who can't defend themselves. I lost it.

I slammed open the car door with such force that the bastard fell to the ground, giving me space to get out of the car. I grabbed the fire extinguisher off its hook and slammed it across his ear and face, so he didn't make it to his feet. Oops. He went down again.

I stood ready to punch his face with the extinguisher. He raised his hands, begging me not to hit him. He was already bleeding.

"You ever come near me again, I will not be the one to do the dirty work. I have very nasty friends that will fuck you like a pussy."

He made a noise, inarticulate. I have no idea what he was trying to say. He was sniveling.

"Don't believe it, huh?" I drew back, ready to let the fire extinguisher extinguish him.

"I believe you! What the fuck? I didn't come here to fight." Blood and a broken tooth sprayed out of his mouth. He could hardly talk.

"Ava and Emma are my friends. I don't give a fuck what your business is with them, but if I find out you put your filthy hands on either one of them again, I will hunt you down, and you won't like it when I find you. Got that?"

I lowered the extinguisher down, so it pressed against his pretty nose without pressure.

"I don't want to fuck up your face. It's up to you."

"I hear you," he said. "I would never hurt them."

I threw the extinguisher to the side, got in my car, put my head out the window, and watched the fucker stir in pain. I hate bullies, especially men who bully a woman. He needed stitches. When I broke Danny's jaw, I had felt bad afterward. I didn't feel bad now. I felt pretty good.

"What the fuck is your name?" I asked, raising my voice.

"Jaime," he said. He managed to get himself to a sitting position on the cement inches from my car.

"Jaime, I don't muscle anyone, but I know how. Don't ever fuck with me again, and don't forget what I told you about Ava and Emma. You better treat them like they're made of glass."

I put the car in reverse and drove toward the freeway. I would be late if traffic was fucked going to Riverside where Matt and I were working.

I wanted to call Ava, but I had no time to stop at a payphone.

I left the anger I felt in the parking lot with the jerk who had caused it. I turned the radio on and looked at the clock. I wasn't going to be late. I would have to buy lunch. I had no one to make lunch for me like my mom did when I was living there, though I had what I needed to make sandwiches. I just hadn't thought about it this morning and most mornings.

When I pulled up to the job site, Matt was getting out of his truck, and he was pointing. I didn't know what the gesture meant. I opened the window.

"What happened to your door?"

I slammed on the brakes, got out of the car and that's when I saw the dent the prick had made on my beautiful car. Maybe I'd slammed the door into him harder than I'd thought.

All day long, I was bothered by the damage. I needed to get it fixed right away. After work, I drove home by way of a body shop that had been at Brooklyn and Rowan in East Los Angeles for ages, not that far from my apartment.

The parking lot for the body shop was shared with a Mexican meat market. The body shop had wide entrances, one facing Brooklyn Avenue, the other facing Rowan. The lot was bumper-to-bumper busy, but I could not tell if the traffic was from the market or the body shop. I went inside and paid five dollars for an estimate to repair the door, with a promise that I would get a credit if they did the repairs. The guy did the estimate right there in the parking lot.

"I have the best painter in town," Ramirez said, chewing away at an unlit cigar as he spoke, the cigar dangling between his lips. He was an old guy with lots of lines on his puffy, leathery face showing the hard path his life had taken. His name was embroidered on his dirty shirt. He introduced himself as the shop owner. "I promise a perfect match, or you pay nothing."

Ramirez was a likable guy. I liked him, and I liked his terms.

I made a deal to bring the car Friday after work, and I could pick it up on Sunday.

"I'm here seven days a week," he said. "You will have the car on time, so you don't miss work on Monday."

On Friday, Ramirez had a mechanic drive me to my apartment to drop me off at home after work.

After I took a shower, I called Ava. Emma answered.

"She has company for a while," Emma said. "I'm on my P if you only want company. We can kick back, watch TV, and I can do things to you, no charge."

"I got no wheels until Sunday afternoon. Come over, and we'll order a pizza and watch TV."

"Poor baby. Where's the car? Getting that dent fixed?"

"Yeah, that prick."

"He got thirteen stitches."

"I heard."

"I'm on my way."

Emma and I were laid back, watching TV, and necking like teens might do at the movies.

"Stay the night," I said.

"I'd love that," she said.

Ava came over twice, each time grabbing a slice and rushing back to get ready for another job. It was Friday night, and Jaime was keeping Ava busy from his home, wherever that was. Jaime normally met up with new clients to take them to the back entrance, but with him out of it, Ava had to wait in front of the building and walk them through the parked cars to the back door of their apartment.

Emma and I hugged and spooned. I went to sleep like that, spooning, fighting memories of Selena. I woke up enjoying the feeling of a woman lying next to me in the morning. I didn't care that she had red hair or that I couldn't have sex with her. We exchanged morning breath kisses.

Emma went home to shower, promising to return.

I heard knocking at the door and turned off the water. I stepped out of the shower and opened the door with a towel wrapped around my midsection.

Emma was standing there with hair as wet as mine, and a plate covered with a paper towel.

She walked in and put the plate on my kitchen table.

"Breakfast, G. Eat your heart out." Before I could thank her, she kissed me.

"I'll be back," she said and was gone again.

I sat at the kitchen table to remove the paper towel, revealing a huge omelet with four slices of bacon and two slices of wheat toast on the side.

The omelet was like something from a restaurant, ham chopped up in small pieces, cheese, and even jalapenos. I'm not an egg eater, then or now, but I loved it. I was righteously surprised with the breakfast plate.

There I was in my kitchen with only a towel wrapped around me, and for the first time, I used my new dish soap and sponge to wash the plate to have it clean and ready for Emma. I put on shorts and a shirt and white tennis shoes. No socks. Everything was new, worn for the first time, part of the department store locker thing.

I felt energized. I felt happy.

Emma came back barefoot in white shorts and a white shirt. When she smiled, I admired her perfect teeth, which I don't think I'd noticed before.

"I'm glad you're here," I said.

"I'm not leaving until you show me the door," she laughed.

I pointed. "White shorts. Living dangerously?"

She checked herself out first. "Oh, you're bad," she said.

"I was kidding," I said.

"I got it all under control," she said. "White shorts are safe."

We took our accustomed places on the sofa, TV on.

"Ava had a long night," she said. "She wants to sleep till noon.

She offered to drive me anywhere I wanted in the white Pinto she shared with Ava. It was parked a few spaces from my car.

"When you get hungry, we can go eat somewhere. If Ava is free, the three of us can go."

I really like Emma and Ava.

She glanced toward the kitchen. "Fuck, if you had cooking stuff, I could make you anything you want."

"What are you a chef or something?" I kidded.

"Short-order cook at Denny's for three years."

"So, that's why the omelet was out of this world."

"Aw, anyone can throw together an omelet. I cook up a storm for Ava and me."

I smiled at my friend. I felt close to her. I can be a softy, but no, I never married her.

As Emma spent Saturday with me, Ava came and went many times.

I'd had two beers. Emma sat beside me on the sofa, her legs across my lap. She rolled a joint and smoked about a third of it. Possession of marijuana in any amount was illegal, but I didn't judge. Even with all that I'd been through, I didn't know how to inhale a cigarette, much less a joint. I tried it, probably not hard enough.

Ava came to the front door, let herself in, and sat on the couch as she drank a cup of coffee that she'd brought with her. She hung out with us for about three minutes, then looked at her watch and ran out the door. I noticed she was wearing a different sundress than she'd had on before, and that her hair was damp.

Based on my observations, I asked Emma, "Is Ava showering after every time she sees someone?"

Emma laughed at my question.

"She douches every time, and if there is time, she showers. So, do I. Doesn't feel right to fuck one guy, then fuck another without a shower. Not all dude's fuck. If they want something else, those are easy clean up."

"How many guys has Ava gone through, yesterday and today?"

"It depends," she said. "Jaime spaces them out depending on how much he charges the customer, and he calls me or Ava to tell us. I've done 10 in 10 hours."

"That has to hurt."

"It's a job. I make more money on a bad day than I did cooking for a whole week."

I gave her an understanding look. What could I say? She lit up the joint again. I didn't smoke, but I might have had a contact high. Hanging out with Emma was like she was my girlfriend.

On Sunday, while Ava was working, Emma took me to get my car. My Impala was waiting for me, looking brand new right outside the body shop. Emma waited while I went to check it out. First, I got out of the car and looked at the repair, then opened the door to see if the mechanic had left a mess inside. He hadn't.

Ramirez came out wearing a big smile, cigar hanging out of his mouth. He looked like he had slept all weekend in the coveralls I'd last seen him in.

"What you think, kid?"

"I am impressed and thankful. It's perfect. It looks like it did the day I drove it off the lot."

I handed him one hundred and fifty dollars in cash[3] and didn't ask him for the five-dollar credit I had coming. I shook his hand.

"You the man, Ramirez."

He had a deep throaty laugh that struck me as unique. Ramirez did this funny bow. When I thanked him for the great

---

3. Adjusted for inflation, $150.00 in 1963 is equal to $1,267.96 in 2020.

job on my Impala, he bowed with a grin that only a happy man could put on his face.

I wish I had that grin. Even when I laugh, people ask me why I'm frowning.

* * *

I went back to the Pinto. Emma rolled her window down.

"Car looks great," I said.

Emma looked uneasy. "It does look great," she agreed. "Ava and I were talking about your car situation. We feel guilty that you exploded at him over us."

"Sneaking up to my car and ramming his finger at my window was his doing, not yours. Please don't feel guilty. He did that all by himself." I kissed her.

I had some bills in my right pocket. I pulled the money out and put it in her hand.

"G, no, I didn't do anything. No."

I kissed her again.

"Look, you aren't working right now. This will help buy beer or something."

She unfolded the money. Her jaw dropped, and she looked from the bills to me.

"No. Two hundred? No way."

I kissed her again.

"I can afford it," I said. "My feelings will be hurt if you don't take it as a gift."

Her eyes got wet, and she wiped them.

"Ava is not working tonight," she said. "We can go to dinner or something, my treat."

"See you back at the house. I'm going to stop and gas up."

She blew me a kiss, put the pinto in gear, and pulled into traffic.

Until I stepped back, I didn't notice that Ramirez was still by my car watching with a big grin. I'm pretty sure he only saw the kisses.

Chapter 9
Sophia

I decided to attend the party that the massage lady had invited me to. It was a Friday, and Ava and Emma would be busy. On my way, I stopped at a flower shop, got appropriate flowers, and wrote the graduate's name on the card. Congratulations, Sophia.

Cathy answered the door and greeted me like an old friend.

"The flowers are beautiful. Come in and let me introduce you to Sophia."

Cathy took my arm and escorted me into a room crowded with strangers, mostly around my age, plus a cluster of people who had to be Sophia's family. The music was loud enough to vibrate the walls but not so loud that there were complaints, at least not that I heard or saw.

Cathy pointed out Sophia to me, and I couldn't help but notice her striking good looks. She was so pretty. I glanced in her direction, and when our eyes met, time seemed to pause. Her hazel eyes mirrored my own, creating an instant connection.

Sophia had dancing feet. I'm lucky that Pi had taught me how to bebop at Hollenbeck Park while his homies looked on. No one dared to make fun of him. He was a great dancer. I never much liked to dance, but I knew how.

I danced with Sophia more than once. She said she lived with her grandparents. Her parents had passed away when she was a little girl. I asked for no details. I knew no one when I got there, but before I left, I had met everyone. There were no homies, but still, we all lived in East Los Angeles. Only Sophia and I came from Boyle Heights. Sounds nice but it's still East Los Angeles. After the party, I took Sophia's number home with me.

The next day, I called and invited her to eat. I took Sophia to my favorite spot in Chinatown. The host seated us where I used to sit with Alicia and, before her, Selena. The busy, crowded, noisy restaurant around us disappeared as we focused on each other.

"Do you have to study for your cosmetology license?"

"I have my license. The school requires you to pass the state exam before you graduate."

"Bad for those that flunk the test and don't get proof they paid to get the education. Good for you because you passed."

"Thanks. Good point," Sophia said, "I never thought of that."

My family consisted of just my mom, my dad, Leonard, a brother in Mexico that I hadn't seen in years, and my sister, Mary. I had a feeling my dad in Douglas, Arizona, had written me off once more. In contrast, although Sophia had lost her parents, she was surrounded by a close-knit family that offered her abundant support.

"Are you planning to work at a salon?"

"I start full-time in a week. I've been working weekends at a salon owned by a family friend. When I get enough experience, I want to get my place."

I didn't tell her about spending time in jail or getting married and divorced twice, at least not that night. I told her about work.

"You have an interesting job. No wonder you have such a beautiful car."

"You can drive it anytime," I said.

Sophia brightened. "Thanks. I'm a good driver."

"I bet you are. Do you have a car?"

"I have a Mustang."

"Nice. I love Mustangs."

"Me too. It's small for short people like me."

"You're not so short," I said.

Sophia smiled. "Thanks."

George J Hatcher

* * *

Thanks to cosmetology, Sophia could do her makeup and hair in all sorts of ways: far out, casual, serious, any way you can imagine. There never was very much makeup on her face except when she was playing around. She was funny and shy. If anything, she was way too nice about everything.

Her family celebrated every weekend at a different house. I went with her. They made me feel like I was part of the family

Her grandfather, Jesse, was a short man who installed floor tile. His biceps and hands were strongly muscled, thanks to the hard work of his job. He was a strong dude. I hand-wrestled him a number of times. He was in a floor tile layers' union and never let anyone forget it. The union meant a lot to him. As a journeyman ten times over, Jesse made good money. On the job, he wore knee pads and used a four-wheel dolly. His work included big commercial jobs where he laid out thousands of feet of vinyl tile. He told me more than once that he was waiting for the day his knees would give out. Then he'd have to give up laying floor tile.

He was a cool person until he started drinking beer. Every day after getting home, he drank. He also drank during the weekly parties and was happy-go-lucky at all the family gatherings.

During one party, when he was well-lit, he started on me. He would kick my ass if I ever mistreated Sophia. I didn't disagree with him. The mistake Jesse made was that he poked my chest to add ferociousness to drunken intimidation. Not one poke. Not two. He did it seven times before I exploded. I punched him, and he went flying backward. He landed on top of a console television. No one was watching, but his wife came to his rescue. She and Sophia shoved me out of the way, then they checked to make sure he was okay. He was. I was not drunk, nor did I have an anger problem.

I just don't appreciate being poked and intimidated. He got so close to my face when he was jabbing me that he sprayed me with his beery spittle.

For five days, I didn't call Sophia, and she didn't call me. In the meantime, I found refuge with Emma and Ava and work. You'd think I would erupt at Matt for being as rough as he was, but I respected him too much. He screamed, flung his eyeglasses to kingdom come, and even jumped up and down on his cap, but he never poked or touched me.

Ava and Emma were not hot tamales. There is nothing attractive about a tamale. They were just hot. The only quality time I spent with them was during that time of the month when they were off work. I liked the company, especially if two days of it were on a weekend.

On one such weekend, Ava asked, "Are you serious about Sophia?"

"I don't know if I'm serious," I replied. "What is serious?"

"I know her. That girl's been waiting to date for a long time," Ava said. "She told me herself no one was getting in her panties unless there was a marriage."

"I been out with her at least seven times, including the parties they throw every week. I haven't even tried to get in her panties."

"I can see you aren't serious about her," Ava said and kissed me.

Chapter 10
Lessons Unlearned

Sophia and I were married at the downtown courthouse with no promises to her grandparents to get married by the Catholic church like they wanted us to. By then, Sophia knew everything about my life. She told me she didn't care about my past. The only condition she threw at me was that she didn't want to live next door to Ava and Emma. She didn't badmouth them, but she knew what they did for a living.

"Don't tell me if you don't want to," Sophia said. "Did you do it with either one of them?"

"I can lie and say I didn't."

"I don't want you to lie," Sophia said. "Thanks for telling me."

* * *

Sophia wanted a place away from anyone, which may or may not have meant Emma and Alicia. "I don't care if it's a tiny place," Sophia said.

I told Ava I was moving.

"I should have never suggested you call Cathy to come over and massage you," Ava said with a frown.

I kissed Ava long and hard, then I did the same to Emma.

"Hey, it's not like I'm dead," I said. "I love you both. You've been so good to me."

Ava kissed me first.

"I hope it works for you. Sophia is lucky."

"For sure." Emma moved close to kiss me again. "A hunk is what you are." She hugged me tightly, and I hugged her back.

It broke my heart to let go of my apartment. A part of me wished to hold onto it while also finding a house for Sophia and me. That's simply how I felt.

"Don't think for a moment that I wasn't in love with Sophia. She was so different from my other wives that I never doubted our marriage would be anything but successful. It wasn't like in the movies where you propose, and the girl goes wild with joy, wrapping her arms around you and shouting YES. Sophia didn't say yes right away. She told me she needed time to think about it and didn't even glance at the engagement ring. Imagine that. I took her hesitation as a no, and accepting no has always been difficult for me. But she grew on me, and I kept trying."

* * *

I had a vacation coming, but I didn't expect much from Matt. He didn't care about rules. I told him I'd gotten married again and wanted a week off to honeymoon. I was surprised when he said, "I hope this one works out for you, kid. See you in a week."

He pulled out his wallet, peeled out three hundred-dollar bills, and handed them to me. "Here's your wedding gift."

"Matt, no way. No gift necessary."

"Kid, we have the afternoon in front of us to work. Don't upset me. Take the money."

It reminded me of my running battle with Emma and Ava to take the money.

"This will go a long way in Mexico," I said to Matt. "Thank you from both of us."

Matt grunted.

* * *

Our plans were to fly to Acapulco for our honeymoon, a unique experience for us. I had never taken Selena to Acapulco, so the memory would be Sophia's and mine. In Acapulco, we did what happy newlyweds do. We had fun. Hours and hours on the beach and we went out every night, which meant a place where there was dancing because this lady loved to dance.

Sophia had a stunning figure and looked fantastic in a bathing suit. She selected three sexy suits, each form-fitting but tasteful. One featured a cut-out that revealed some skin, yet it was more modest compared to what Selena or Alicia might wear. Although Twiggy had not yet become a fashion icon, Sophia could effortlessly transform her appearance with makeup, reminiscent of Twiggy's versatility. While Sophia wasn't the tall, slender type, she had her own unique magic when it came to changing her look.

* * *

Sophia had some free time during the day and could almost make her own work hours. While I was at work, she and her grandmother found us a tiny brand-new duplex on Eighth Street near Lorena in East Los Angeles. The neighborhood was the best part of the deal. The kitchen was tiny, the living room was tiny, the bedroom was tiny, and closet space for my clothes was non-existent. I took most of my stuff from my apartment to my mother's house. Sophia was okay with the apartment. I was okay with it because I had nothing to do with finding it, so her family couldn't blame me for Sophia living in a closet. Both of us worked during the day, so maybe size didn't matter. We had no yard, no garage, only a carport for our two cars. If anyone came to visit, they had to park on the street. The rent was seventy dollars a month.

I bought a color television at my first opportunity. No one in Sophia's family had a color TV, and you might think that a color TV was an open invitation. Our place was too small to host more than two people other than us.

I was doing great at work. I had three raises in the first year and union-scale entitlements as long as I kept advancing at work and in trade school. My hourly wages were great, and Matt was still sharing bonuses when he got them.

    I drank a lot of beer, but thanks to daily jogging and Matt's vigorous work ethic, I was slim and trim. I didn't take to hard liquor. Sophia exercised, but wouldn't jog with me. Her thing was aerobics to music. While I jogged in the early morning, she did thirty minutes of jumping and dancing and it kept her looking nice.

When Sophia announced she was pregnant, it reminded me of how I felt when my sister Mary was born. Mary had been the only baby I really knew. Soon, I would have a child of my own.

Sophia's grandmother was involved in our life like you wouldn't believe. I'm not saying that was bad or had anything to do with me leaving for a spell. Grandma had Sophia quit work. She wanted her to take it easy, so there would be no complications. I figured it was nonsense that she had to move. We didn't give up the apartment. It just was left without us. Sophia went home with her grandmother, and I went back to the basement at my mom's, with conditions. I told my mother that I was not going to eat dinner there, that I wasn't going to be checking in and out, and to pretend I was a stranger, a tenant living downstairs.

My mom urged me to go back home. She had a broken record on the topic and kept reminding me that Sophia was pregnant.

"Mom, I'm not moving in with her grandmother. She left. I didn't leave."

We were apart for a while. When we got back together, I couldn't remember what had caused the separation. The tiny duplex was history. We found a three-bedroom house to rent in the City of Commerce, not far from where my ex-wife Alicia and Clara had lived. Clara still lived there with Danny, but my ex moved in with Paul.

* * *

The baby was due in October, during my birthday month, but she didn't make it full term. My little Judy was born at seven months and didn't come home with us immediately. I was worried sick because she was in an incubator for days and days, looking so frail, hooked up to all that equipment. It was terrifying, that tiny life hanging in the balance. She was so frail and helpless, and we were helpless to do anything but endure the torture of waiting. Sophia stayed at the hospital and urged me not to miss work. She assured me that Judy would pull through.

Finally, Judy came home, a lovely baby with hazel eyes.

Having a baby is wonderful but stressful. The crying at night and all the extra stuff that goes with taking care of an infant can get you down. It's not like either of us were baby experts, or, like they say, babies don't come with a manual. I was really happy, but I felt beaten up. No sleep for me at night, then during the day, I had Matt to deal with.

I'd get home, and Sophia's grandmother would be over. Thank God for that because she knew her way around babies and was a lot of help to Sophia and me. Then Grandpa Jesse came over. Grandma and Grandpa used the third bedroom to be close to Sophia and the baby. That pushed my panic button. They moved in, and I moved out.

Sophia said, "If you are getting anxious living here with us, rent the bachelor apartment you had and move there."

I went back to the old apartment complex. The apartment I had was rented out. My new apartment was on the first floor across from Emma and Ava. When I looked out my window from the living room, I had the pool as before, but now I was in direct view of their front door.

I didn't move back to the apartment to be near my friends. I moved back because it was familiar turf. Like many people, I don't like change. I disliked being alone, but I liked the unlimited freedom that came with it.

Even though it didn't happen as fast as my first two marriages, I told myself that marriage to Sophia was another hurried decision. In the first two marriages, I thought of marriage as being the only way not to lose them. Sophia was my third marriage. I was looking to settle down.

* * *

I visited my wife and child. Ironically, they were still living in the house I was paying rent on. "I should move in," I said. "I miss you. Do you miss me?"

Sophia hugged me. Judy was too young to know what was going on.

"I do miss you," Sophia said. "But you can't stop my grandparents from coming over to help me like they do."

"Honey, they don't come over to help you. They've moved in. If I want to walk around in my underwear in my own house, I can't do it because your grandfather will think I'm being disrespectful to your grandmother. He told me that once."

"He was kidding, and you know it."

"He wasn't kidding."

"I'll talk to him if you want to move back. I promise you can run around in your underwear, skivvies as you call them." She laughed. I kissed her. I was considering it.

"If you come back, you have to give up the apartment."

"I'm not giving up my apartment," I said. "How do I know this will work if I come back and it doesn't work?"

Sophia was cool about it. She made a funny face, gave me a poke on the chest, then she said, "George, come visit anytime you want for as long as you want, but don't move back. I can't handle you. If you can't get everything you need from me, why be with me?"

A couple of days later, I came back and stayed with Sophia, my daughter, and Sophia's grandparents. After about two weeks, Sophia was already pushing me to get rid of the apartment, and I hadn't even been back to the apartment.

Chapter 11
Spreading Out

I kept trying to get back to Sophia. I'd go home, and soon after I was there, we argued about her grandparents being there and me having my own apartment. I knew our marriage was falling apart. Neither Sophia nor I believed in staying together for the children's sake.

"Stop coming back on account of your guilt trip over Judy. She's going to be just fine. We know you love her."

I chuckled that time. "What you're saying is that I should split again."

"Yeah," she said. "Split. Vamoose. Skedaddle."

I went back to my apartment. Anyway, I preferred jogging in Monterey Hills more than where the rented house was located.

* * *

I found a tiny scrape on the trunk lid of my car. It was small but ugly and perplexing, and I couldn't figure out how it got there. Maybe someone else would have let it go. Maybe someone else would have thought it was too small to mess with it. But every time I opened the trunk, there it was, screaming at me, and it hurt. One afternoon after work, I drove the little scrape to Ramirez's body shop. Traffic from the job site was always a bear. It was after five. I didn't know how late they stayed open.

From the Rowan Avenue side, the shop looked closed. I almost drove away until I noticed that the Brooklyn Avenue accordion gates were half open. I parked and walked in.

"Hello," I said, first in my speaking voice, then a couple of times, getting a little louder each time. I always like bright lights. At the apartment, I turn on all the lights and still complain the place is not bright enough. There was hardly any light in here. It was getting dark outside, and the lighting was terrible. It took a minute for my eyes to adjust. There was still more gloom than gleam, and I had been better off before my eyes adjusted. I hadn't been inside before, and this was not how I'd pictured it. I had expected an orderly shop, everything in its place, the clientele's cars in some kind of organization. The place was big and a mess. Tools were scattered and abandoned where they'd last been used. The lighting was terrible, very dim, with only a couple of high ceiling lights, not all of them with working tubes. It wasn't empty by any means, but most of the cars that were parked here and there looked rusted in place, abandoned from an earlier time. Maybe some were parts cars, or maybe they were customers who never came back. The air stank of rancid oil, mildew from a leak somewhere, cigar smoke, and disuse. Paper bags, oil cans, oil rags, and miscellaneous garbage collections trickled over the sides of rusted-out barrels. I stepped over debris and made my way toward a grimy, tired-looking desk in the corner, stacked high with papers and folders and surrounded by a precariously leaning tower of parts boxes.

No one had answered my call. I was about to leave when a familiar face came through the accordion doors. Ramirez carried a small paper bag and had that ever-present cigar stub gripped in his teeth, an inch of ash on the end. When he saw me, he smiled around the cigar.

"Hey kid, I remember you by that car out there."

"Hey Ramirez," I said. I knew his face from the last time he fixed the car, but there was something else familiar about him. "If you shut down, I can come back. I have this tiny scrape I want to take care of."

His coveralls were deeply stained with grease and dirt. I think they may have once been white, but that was a long while ago. The v of his shirt exposed a mass of salt and pepper chest hair, not the most professional look I'd ever seen, but he had a jovial manner that instantly put me at ease. He vigorously wiped his free hand on the seat of his pants before extending it to me.

"Good to see you again, kid." He glanced at his watch, shook his arm a couple of times, and put it to his ear as if to check if it was ticking. "I'm not closed until I go home." He laughed a booming laugh, and I realized who he reminded me of.

He reminded me of an older, shorter, uglier, fatter version of Pancho, my former uncle-in-law in Juarez. He had the same leathery skin stained dark from years of sun exposure, and there was just something about him beyond the fondness for alcohol.

"Let me pour myself a quick little toddy, and I'll check the car. Can I pour you one?"

"I'm driving," I said, "but thanks."

I was almost expecting El Presidente to appear, but from the bag, he took a pint of Early Times and some paper cups like the ones in my bathroom at home.

"One ain't going to make you drunk, and besides, it's after closing time, five o'clock, time I open the bag every day."

"Thanks, I'm good."

The expression on his puffy, wrinkled face was comical.

Who in this dump had worked on my car and made it look perfect? I'm not a gambler, but I'd wager it wasn't Ramirez.

Liquor sloshed over the rim as he poured it into one of those small cups. He took a couple of long, hard swallows.

"Ah, that feels good!"

He smacked his lips, then walked over to the desk and picked up a clipboard with a pad on it.

He balanced his cup on the hood of my car. "The going rate is five for an estimate. Give you credit if you let me do the job."

"Ramirez, I don't need a written estimate. Tell me how much."

"You do. It's only five bucks."

"I know the drill. I'll give you the five bucks. How much?"

Ramirez ignored me as he scribbled on his pad.

I left him.

Further in, where it was partly lit, I saw a makeshift paint spray booth covered with canvas.

Ramirez was older, and this shop was much bigger, but I felt a wave of nostalgia. Ramirez, his toddy, his shop, his paint booth. Everything reminded me of Pancho and Juarez. What would Pancho have done with a huge space like this? The building had room for more than forty cars-at least. It would if all the junk cars were removed.

George J Hatcher

While working with Matt, I had been thinking all along about what I would do if I went into business for myself. Owning an air conditioning business was only in my wheelhouse because that's what I was doing, and I always dreamed of being on the top of the food chain. I thought about that because that competitive part of me was up for giving WESPAC a run for its money, but I didn't have any special affinity to the profession. I was never able to dream small. Always the rogue dreams would tease me, then I'd put them back in my pocket and focus on the job at hand. A good part of me is always geared to seeking out a good opportunity.

Working with Matt, I learned to begin a job by organizing the essentials. I looked at the room around me, remembering

Pancho. Pancho was a craftsman with a tiny hole in the wall where he painted cars. He wasn't a role model by any means, but he'd given me a rudimentary look at what the business entailed. What would I do if I were going to fix it? Clean it out, sell the scrap, get it in order, fix the paint booth up. I got caught up in the planning. New lights, spray booth. I thought of the Earl Scheib ads and pictured their immaculate spray booth and the infrared drying booth that baked the paint dry fast.

The inspiration was coming at me almost too fast. The only thing wrong with Ramirez's shop was its condition. The location was good. Busy intersection. Busy meat market next door. New Safeway across the street. For me, Ramirez's place was a greenhouse of blooming ideas.

"A hundred and fifty 'bananas,' and I'll have it looking like new."

It took me a second to follow his words. I was too deeply into planning. Mechanically, I walked back to him. I handed over the five bucks without looking at the estimate.

He put the money in his pocket, then gestured over his shoulder to the junked cars. He rolled the estimate up into a cylinder and pointed with it vaguely toward the cars.

"I saw you looking back there. Anything you might need? Give you a hell of a deal on anything here," he said between swallows.

"I've been thinking of going into this kind of business." It was true. I had been considering it for an entire thirty seconds.

Ramirez grinned broadly. "Do you got the bread to do it?"

"Depends on what it takes."

I met his eyes squarely. We stared at one another. I heard the traffic outside, the annoying hum of a lame light fixture, and some distant ping of something hitting the warehouse, and saw the pulse of the vein in Ramirez's neck and the twitching of his Adam's apple.

Ramirez gestured toward his desk. "Come over here and have a drink. I'll let you pick my brain."

My heart beat hard and fast as I followed him to the ancient wooden chair opposite the desk. The padded armchair exploded dust as he plopped down, covering his paper cup till the storm passed. I sneezed twice but thought nothing of it.

A wild idea was sparking to life inside my head.

When the dust settled, he topped off his cup and poured a half cup of Early Times for me.

"I'd offer you a cigar, but I don't have anymore," he said.

The core of excitement within me expanded. It was almost six. From where I was sitting, I could see heavy rush-hour traffic at the intersection. The meat market next door was packed. My car was boxed in on all sides. I'd only need a fraction of those people.

"I got a gold mine here. I messed up and gave credit to people, and they didn't pay me. I been here more than ten years."

He didn't say outright that he wanted to sell, but as he talked, I became convinced that's what he wanted to do.

"Been here too long. Burned out. Lost the fire I had ten years ago when I started. This place was mobbed back then."

"Looks big enough to have all kinds of departments." The paint booth was the only department I recognized.

"Sure thing, kid. Bodywork, painting, mechanical, transmission, upholstery...used to have them all. Only thing I ain't never had is a real spray booth. If I had one...."

He emptied his cup, exhaled loudly in appreciation, poured himself more liquor, leaned back in his seat, and put his feet on the desk. I pounced.

"Think you'd ever want to sell this place?" I asked.

His grin reappeared. "Got a gold mine here, kid. I don't know."

"What kind of a lease do you have on this place? How much is the rent?"

"Got no lease. The old lady that owns the place don't believe in them. Rent is up to two seventy-five[1], now. Ten years ago, it was twenty-five bucks. But the old bag would never give up a lease. Even the meat market next door doesn't have one, and them brothers are worth a million bananas, at least."

My eyebrows shot up. The rent was dirt cheap. There had to be at least eight thousand square feet in the building.

"But without a lease, place isn't worth much," I challenged.

"Nonsense, kid. Old lady Goldberg is a rich old bag from Beverly Hills. She will live to be a hundred. She don't want this place. She has dozens of rentals. Hundreds." He burped, and his eyes drifted shut for a second. "Thousands," he said softly, eyes still shut.

I stared at him, but my mind was cranking up a storm. One of his eyes popped open, and he gave me a wink. "Interested?" he slurred.

I snapped to attention. "You mean you want to sell?"

"You got ten thousand bananas?"

"I'd give you a thousand. More than a thousand, if there was a lease."

"Five thousand would take care of it, kid."

"Fifteen hundred."

Ramirez laughed and poured himself another drink. "Place is a gold mine, kid. You're going to blow the deal of a lifetime."

I turned in my chair, surveying Ramirez's kingdom and gold mine. I didn't see much gold. It was very dark outside, and darker inside, but I hadn't seen much worth keeping when the light had been marginally better. What was there to keep? The rusted-out trash barrels? A couple hundred dollars worth of

---

1. Adjusted for inflation, $275.00 in 1962 is equal to $2,355.59 in 2020

worn-out automotive tools. A compressor that ... Half of a compressor?

"What about equipment? I don't see much."

Ramirez snorted. "Jacks, tools, ten years' worth of everything you need. My bodyman and my mechanic each come with his own tools. The painter counts on me for spray guns and compressor I have all that. You saw the paint job on your door. Got a good painter."

"Could be I'd pay two thousand."

"Four thousand, cash."

"No way." I shook my head.

"Three thousand. Not a nickel less."

"I don't have it. If I had it, I'd have no money to do what is needed in this place to get it going. I'd be like you, wanting to sell and no one buying."

He slapped the desk again, smashing his cup. I could tell it was an accident by his tragic expression. His lip curled into a pout as he picked it up and tried getting back into shape, but it didn't work. He crushed it in his palm, tossed it in the trash, and pulled out a fresh cup. He filled it and passed it under his nose, breathing in the scent of Early Times.

"Two thousand," he sighed deeply, then said, almost like it was an afterthought, "but the equipment is another thousand."

"Two thousand[2] for everything."

I held out my hand.

Ramirez leaned forward but didn't take my hand. Beads of sweat formed on his grimy forehead and cleaned a trail down to his brows. He looked bewildered.

I almost felt sorry for him. I slowly moved my hand down on the desktop, his eyes following like I had a pot of gold in there that he'd never get his hands on.

---

2. Adjusted for inflation, $2,000.00 in 1962 is equal to $17,131.60 in 2020.

"Look, kid, the truth is that I owe the old lady three months' rent. There's no way I can pay her and let you have the place for two gees." He belched. "Pay the back rent I owe, and we have a deal."

"You were setting me up."

"Three times two seventy-five ain't nothing, kid. Place is a gold mine."

He did not look like the owner of a gold mine, but he'd admitted the fire in his belly was gone. Mine was just beginning. I was more excited than I'd ever been. This was fate dropping a real opportunity right in my lap.

"If you're as serious as I am, give me the landlady phone number to verify what you owe and how much the rent is going to be from here on."

After hesitating for a moment, Ramirez reached for his drink and took a sip before putting on his reading glasses. He proceeded to open a drawer in his desk, which emitted a shrill, eerie noise akin to a wounded creature. A simple application of WD-40 would have easily remedied the situation. From the drawer, he retrieved a tattered phone book. He patted his chest pockets and pant pockets, then found the rolled-up estimate on the desk, flattened it out, and flipped it to copy a number from the book onto the back.

I put it in my pocket. That was too easy. Maybe Ramirez was drunk, but he didn't look drunk as drunk as he'd seemed a few minutes before. He seemed more satisfied than drunk.

I pictured myself as the owner of that large establishment. I could earn big bucks to take care of my daughter. I could give Sophia money, so they were secure. I could afford to travel someday and get the big house and primo cars that had been tempting me my whole life.

"The love this place needs are more than I got," I said, getting up.

Ramirez lurched to his feet, his face tragically disappointed and shocked at the same time.

"But-"

"I'll be back, Ramirez. I want you totally sober if we strike a deal. I'm in a different business. I'm in construction with a promising career. I don't want to jump that fast. I'm not ready to make a deal tonight."

"We just had a deal for two thousand."

"We did. Then you threw in the three months past due rent. Doesn't matter. It's not the past due rent. I need to digest this."

I've learned this about myself: I have a tendency to jump too fast. I jumped to get married three times, and I was down three failures.

Selena was my fault. I had nothing to offer her. I had her living in the back room of the business.

I took Alicia to my mom's basement.

I put Sophia in that tiny place, then in the three bedroom that had nothing in it except what her grandparents put there. I was not the world's best provider. And Sophia was just too nice for me.

"You seem like a smart kid," he said. "Don't you wait too long. Four months over-due rent, and we may both get fucked out of this place."

I shook his hand.

"I got it, Ramirez. I promise, I'll be back."

I started to walk away, stopped, and turned around; he was still at his desk.

"If I make a deal, you need to stick around and teach me how to do estimates and the business in general."

"Kid, for two fifty a week, I'll be here and teach you everything I know."

"We'll talk but, I'm not paying you two-fifty a week to stick around as a teacher."

"Next time you come, bring cash," Ramirez said, laughing.

I don't think he was laughing at me. I think either he hadn't seen cash in a while, or he was cheering to the possibility of foisting his bills on me.

I made it to the door.

"How old are you, kid?" he yelled.

"Twenty-one," I yelled back.

I heard the laugh.

I made up my mind right there and then that the shop was mine.

* * *

From behind my steering wheel, I looked up through my windshield. The shop's signs were weathered, fading. Not a single light outside illuminated them.

The meat market's signs lit up the entire parking lot, but not spectacularly like I would have it. Across the street, Safeway's tall famous logo blazed like the sun from atop the pole. It was like night had fallen everywhere except on the new Safeway building and its giant parking lot. I liked the grandness of this huge building with two big entrances on the corner I knew by heart, with a busy intersection. Safeway bought out a bunch of homes and apartments to build a monster market with way too much parking in that location for a reason. If it was good enough for Safeway, it was good enough for me.

The body shop was hiding its potential like a red-headed stepchild, unwanted, unloved, unknown. But it was surrounded by thriving businesses and an endless cycle of traffic.

The rent sounded like a steal, providing that Ramirez was telling the truth.

* * *

I decided to get dinner. Shakey's Pizza on Atlantic Boulevard was a ten-minute walk from my apartment, a newer place filled with people my age who eat pizza and drink draft beer from a broad and international selection. I sat at the only empty table in the place and ordered a small pizza and a Coors. I stuck to Coors. Every time I held a Coors, I thought of Christine and the guy in the ad. The girl who served me had not asked for my ID. Now that I was twenty-one, I was anxious to show off my driver's license, even though it was not the best picture I ever took.

I was close to home, and I didn't plan on drinking more than two. This was the first time I sat down to eat instead of ordering delivery since I was there for the first time with Ava and Emma. No dancing or entertainment, but music boomed throughout.

I'd know tomorrow if the landlady's phone number was real. I'd have to call her from a payphone near work. I'd have to tell Matt it was a huge emergency.

If I went through with this, what would I tell Matt? What would the Union say? What about the people who moved me up the list so fast? What would I tell my boss at WESPAC?

I could already picture Matt going off about all the time he spent training me shot to hell. He might take a punch at me. If he did, I wouldn't hit back.

Fuck.

The absolute prettiest girl in the world saved me from my thoughts when she delivered my pizza.

"My name is Olivia. I'm your waitress. Looks like your beer is okay. Can I get anything else for you?"

Awestruck, I stared up at her.

Her smile reminded me of Alicia's, gleaming like a toothpaste commercial

"Olivia. This is not a pass. You are gorgeous."

"Thank you. No one has ever told me that before."

"I find that hard to believe."

Olivia had not served me my beer. I started on my pizza, sipped the brew, and watched Olivia take care of a number of tables. She kept coming back to me to check if I was ready for a refill. I had a glass of water in front of me, and she came by and topped it off with a red pitcher of ice.

"Olivia, are you over 18?"

"I'm twenty-one," she said, blushing, both hands on the pitcher.

"Me too," I said. "Sorry for being nosey."

"It's okay. You know my name. What's yours?"

"George. George Hatcher."

I stood up and put my hand out. She transferred the pitcher to her left hand, and we shook hands. She showed me the smile, and I sat down.

"You live in Monterey Park?"

"I do. I live a ten-minute walk from here. Four minutes by car."

Olivia laughed.

I wondered why I didn't come out like this more often.

Chapter 12
Eastland Auto Center

My phone rang, waking me from a dead sleep. The clock by my bed read 5:05. I managed to grab the phone by the third or fourth ring.

"I got a bad ingrown nail and can barely walk. Going to Podiatrist." Matt said, no good morning or hello.

"I can work on my own," I said in the dark with my eyes still shut. "Sorry about your toe."

"Union rules. You can't be on a job alone yet."

"I understand. What do you want me to do?"

"Go back to sleep. Call me tonight, and I'll let you know if we are a go tomorrow."

"I wish your toe well," I said.

Matt hung up.

I had never missed work before. Matt had never missed either, except for that time he went to Paris on vacation.

I had to call Ramirez's landlady today. Other than that, I had the day to myself. I closed my eyes until the alarm rang at the usual five-thirty.

I took my regular jog, thirty minutes on the streets and sidewalks of Monterey Hills. Olivia from Shakey's was on my mind. I already knew what I wanted to do with Olivia. I had her phone number. My plan was to call her Saturday or Sunday on her day off and see what we could do together.

Half a block over from my apartment is a street that goes straight up a hill. Jogging, it feels like a mountain, but it's a hill. Brand new homes were being built on both sides, and gorgeous larger homes were at the top with what had to be spectacular views. Monterey Hills in Monterey Park was like an oasis in the Eastside. Just blocks away on Atlantic Boulevard were grocery stores, banks, drugstores, and shops that had appeared with the development of Monterey Hills. I wanted to be in a financial position to buy property and live a high-end life. I knew becoming a journeyman at the trade I was in, even if I had bonuses and fringes that Matt had, would not take me where I wanted to go.

At nine, I was in my living room, exercised, showered, dressed, and fed. I'd eaten the sandwiches I made the night before to take for lunch.

I took out the car estimate and flattened it face down on my kitchen table. It reeked of cigarette smoke and garage. At least I'd know soon enough if this was a good number. I dialed Mrs. Goldberg. The line was busy.

I thought of calling the girls across the way, but they probably had worked late and were still asleep. I puttered around the kitchen, tossed the paper bag my sandwich had been in, rinsed off the cup and spoon that was in the sink, used them to make a cup of coffee, and then sat down at the table to drink it. Only minutes had passed. Ramirez had said about this woman eating nails for breakfast. How bad could she be?

I dialed Mrs. Goldberg again. This time it rang.

"Who is this?" Her voice quavered, sounding elderly.

Nice way to answer the phone. It didn't strike me yet like she was eating nails.

"This is George Hatcher. Is this Mrs. Goldberg?"

"Depends on who George Hatcher is. Are you a peddler?"

"No, I-"

"Then what do you want?"

She was so abrupt it made me laugh. She definitely didn't put up with any nonsense.

"What did you say?"

I realized that she must be hard of hearing. I raised my voice. "I said, what a wonderful morning it is."

"Listen, you don't have to shout at me."

"I could have some money for you."

"Wonderful. What's the money for?"

"Ramirez's past-due rent. I would rather see you in person to talk."

"Talk about what?"

"About getting you paid."

"If he doesn't pay this time, I am throwing him out. I've been putting up with him for more than ten years, and I'm done being nice!"

She reminded me of Matt. Her tone didn't bother me at all. I wanted to chuckle, but I didn't take the chance of rubbing her the wrong way.

"What I have to say is solid," I said. "I have the money to pay the past due rent."

"What did you say your name was?"

We agreed to meet in Echo Park, where she would be collecting rents between noon and one o'clock.

When I got off the phone, it was like getting off. I mean, I was feverishly excited, like you get on the way to orgasm. I wanted Emma and Ava in the worst way. I considered calling Clara, but her husband might be home. A cold dip seemed a good idea. I've never been a good swimmer -you might remember when I was in the Navy-but to kill time, I put my trunks on and jumped in the pool. When I say I jumped in the pool, I walked down the steps.

A few minutes before noon, I took a quick look around the first floor of the Echo Park apartments. I took a quick look because the inside sent me outside for fresh air. I wondered how people could live like that. Everything was dirty, and the hallways stank of urine and rancid oil. I was waiting on the sidewalk in front by the time an old black limousine pulled up to the curb. An elderly man in an elderly suit climbed stiffly out of the driver's seat and creaked painfully to open the back-right door of the limo.

Mrs. Goldberg and her driver slowly walked toward the building. She wore a striking red dress complemented by a stylish red hat adorned with elegant feathers. Dazzling costume jewelry adorned her—layers of necklaces, sparkling bracelets, and rings on every finger. Her complexion appeared smooth and radiant, giving her a delightful charm that brightened her presence.

The driver carried a battered briefcase that might have belonged to Paul Revere. He followed closely behind Mrs. Goldberg, who came to a halt in front of me. She eyed me from head to toe, not saying a word.

I broke the silence.

"Mrs. Goldberg, I'm George Hatcher."

She leaned on her cane and grimly looked me over.

"So, you're George Hatcher. A very handsome young man. I love your curly hair. What I would pay to have that hair." She smiled at me. "My husband was something like you. He had hair like yours before he got old and lost it."

I was speechless. I never expected her to be complimentary.

"Thank you for the kind words, Mrs. Goldberg."

"Lionel, we don't see young ones with good manners like him anymore, do we?"

"I agree, Mrs. Goldberg," Lionel said in a deep baritone, much more vital than his appearance.

Mrs. Goldberg tapped her cane sharply on the ground and said to me, "Come along while I collect these rents."

We walked up a couple of stairs and into the building. She was shaking off my attempts to help her.

"Tell me," she said, "what are you doing with that drunken reprobate Ramirez?"

I explained my history with Ramirez and followed her around the building as she went door-to-door, all the while counting money, scolding the driver who wrote the receipts and reprimanding the renters who fell short. She knocked on a door, and there was no answer. Her cane loudly joined the attack.

"Open this door, or I'll put a lock on it from the outside!"

Mrs. Goldberg was some tough cookie. To my surprise, the tenant opened the door.

"I'm sorry, Mrs. Goldberg, I was in the shower," her tenant apologized.

"A likely story. I bet you were," Mrs. Goldberg said.

Between bouts with renters, I took the floor. I continued, "I have big plans for your building. I'm going to have it painted, install new light fixtures...." then I'd stop as we reached the next door.

With collecting rent and all, I figured she wasn't listening. But I went on.

"You see, Mrs. Goldberg, without a lease, it wouldn't be smart of me to make such a big investment to improve the building."

She finally responded to me, proving she'd been listening all along. "How much are you paying Ramirez for the place?"

"A fair price," I said, avoiding the issue.

She grunted, reminding me of Matt.

"Anything over a dollar is too much," she said. "He's caused me nothing but grief since I've known him. Never pays on time!"

I found myself sticking up for him. "He probably hasn't been doing too well."

"I suppose. What makes you think you'll do better?"

"I'm going to make it a one-stop auto center with a brand-new look!"

I noticed a tiny smile. The creases at the corners of her mouth turned up.

"What kind of lease are you looking for, young man?"

"At least five years with a five-year option."

She grunted. "I don't like leases."

"But how else can I go in there and invest all this money if I don't have the assurances of a lease?"

"How do I know you'll put in all these improvements if I give you the lease?"

"Because you have my word," I said.

She didn't critique that, but I might have heard a faint chuckle.

When her collections were complete, she allowed me to help her walk downstairs to the street. She had refused my help going up but now leaned heavily on me. The ancient driver followed in silence, holding open the door as she climbed back into the limousine. It had been parked in a reserved shady spot, so the inside of the car was not broiling.

"Get in the car, and we'll see what we can come up with."

The driver turned on the ignition, and the air conditioning came on. The car was beautifully maintained, unlike the building we were parked beside. It had leather upholstery and a spotless interior. It smelled of lemon oil. The limo must have really been something when it was new. It was still something now.

"Close the door," she said, "to cool it off in here."

I did as she asked.

We sat in the car, the AC running. She made her decision.

"Young man, I'm going to let you have the lease you want and hope you aren't another Ramirez."

I was so shocked that I almost fell out of the car.

"Shall I have an attorney draw it up?" I asked. "At my expense, of course."

She waved away the suggestion. "There's a stationery nearby. Wolcott's Stationary. Buy two copies of a lease with an option form, and I'll meet you at this address at three. I'll have finished collecting rent at that building by then." She had a steady hand as she wrote out the address on the back of her business card. She handed it to me.

"I don't know what to say," I said.

"George, you cannot do to me what Ramirez has done for so many years. The rent is three hundred a month for the first year of the lease with annual increases for five years. I need to think of the terms for the option. By the time you meet me at Bunker Hill, I'll have worked it out."

I wanted to kiss her. I wanted to shake her hand. What I did is look straight at her, eye-to-eye. "You won't be sorry," I said.

She looked thoughtful, examining my face. I wondered what she was thinking.

"I'm going to be late," she said briskly like she'd gotten a second wind. "See you at three."

At three sharp, I was at the address, a five-story building. The driver, Lionel, met me outside.

"She's waiting on you in the building manager's office," he said. "Follow me."

The hallways did not stink here. The resident manager's place was a white-walled apartment with one room outfitted as an office. Lionel led me past a small den/kitchen combo where a bookish little woman in round glasses was looking through a stack of folders while she was talking on the phone. I presumed she was the resident manager whose apartment this was but didn't ask. Mrs. Goldberg was sitting in another room in a chair facing the door. There was a small desk with a cup full of writing utensils, a desk set, a fancy looking telephone, and a couple local phone books.

"You are punctual, George. I like that."

"I try to be," I said.

Mrs. Goldberg looked over the forms carefully but quickly, checking every word. She took a carbon from her briefcase and placed it between the lease pages. I was expecting her to hand it over to me to fill out, but instead, she positioned herself over the document.

"Your full name?" she said sharply.

I answered her questions. She expertly filled out the lease form in longhand. That wasn't the only surprise.

"I'm including the meat market next to Ramirez on your lease. They pay five hundred a month and should be paying more. They are excellent tenants and mail the rent to me before the first of the month. Ramirez has never mailed me the rent. I've always had to go get it. Your rent plus the meat market will be eight hundred for the first year, eight-fifty for the second year, nine hundred for the third year, nine-fifty for the fourth year, and a thousand for the fifth year."

I thought she was done. "That sounds-"

She put her finger up and continued. "I have included in the five-year lease that you have an option for five more years, providing you are never late on any of your rental payments, and that you and I agree on the terms of the subsequent five-year lease, which we will negotiate prior to the expiration of the first five years. You have any questions?"

"Is there any particular reason you are including the meat market since they are already good tenants?"

She shrugged, not giving a reason. "I prefer it this way. I know they will continue to pay the rent on time; only they will pay it to you, and you will mail me a check that I will get by the first of the month. You should sublease to them, in writing, and charge them a higher rent than they are paying now. I am happy with the rental amounts I just read off to you."

"Are you saying I can sublease to them for seven hundred a month and if they pay me, that I am only out of pocket a hundred a month?"

"George, you have a master lease on the property. You pay me the rent on time, you collect the meat market's rent, and deal with the headaches they may give you. I don't want to be bothered about a leaking roof or a toilet not working. It's all in the lease. You best be smart and include in the sublease to the market that they will pay for all repairs needed, period. That leaves you to foot the bill only for the body shop."

"I get it," I said. I had been right, thinking she was a smart cookie.

"As for the money part, it is here in writing."

She turned the contract to face me and pointed out on the lease what she had already said. Also, I had to pay first and last month rent, plus eight hundred twenty-five dollars for Ramirez's past-due rent. That would squeeze me because I still needed to pay Ramirez. I would negotiate with the meat market. If they wanted a lease, I would require the first and last month rent on the sublease plus a deposit.

Still, I was smiling deep within.

I signed on the dotted line about six times, and Mrs. Goldberg did too, then I wrote Mrs. Goldberg a check for two thousand four hundred and twenty-five dollars.[1] If I had not had this money in the bank, I would not have been able to make a deal with Mrs. Goldberg, no matter if she liked me. This was business. I didn't ask her if she had other property on the Eastside, but it seemed like it pained her to go out that way to Ramirez. Ramirez had said that she lived in Beverly Hills.

She looked at the check, smiled, and we shook hands across the desk.

She got up, I got up, and when she walked with me toward the door, I said, "Mrs. Goldberg, I would feel really good if I can give you a hug."

Mrs. Goldberg smiled at her driver and then me.

I hugged her and she hugged me for longer than I expected. I was sure her eyes were moist when I helped her out to her car.

I have my soft moments, and I cry. I got all choked up but managed not to tear up. I did not wish to appear weak to someone who did not know me yet.

The driver held the door open, and I helped her in. I spoke to her through the open car door.

"Thanks again, Mrs. Goldberg."

"George, I can tell you are a fine young man. I know you will not let me down."

I looked at her smiling up at me, that pale, old face staring with such confidence and trust in me. I felt the sharp need to tell

---

1. Adjusted for inflation, $2,426.00 in 1962 is equal to $20,780.63 in 2020.

her that I was not a fine young man, but I wanted to be. I wanted to tell her about my checkered past, but I had the contradictory urge that, more than anything, I wanted to be the man she thought I was. I had to be that man, so I could do as I planned and provide for my family. So many people depended on me now. Not just my family, but also Mrs. Goldberg, the guys at the meat market, everyone who worked there, and now, everyone who worked at the shop, now working for me.

I closed the car door without confessing.

I had a drive to succeed in the worst way. I had a daughter now. It didn't matter that we were not living together. I needed to provide for Judy and Sophia.

Mrs. Goldberg waved goodbye as the car pulled away from the curb.

I waved back.

I was concerned about Matt. I didn't want him to be hurting, but I hoped we were not working the next day. I needed more time to deal with the meat market and to organize myself. I had to figure out the money. The shop needed a facelift, and I had no money to swing it.

At a little past four, I got to the body shop and parked my car in the lot. I hoped to find him sober. Ramirez did not open his liquor bag until five, or so he said. I saw workers as I went in. I heard a noise. I saw a bodyman with a grinder working on a car and a mechanic doing something under the hood of an old Ford.

Ramirez grinned big time when he saw me and motioned me over to his desk. I showed him my lease, and he stopped being nice. Why was I surprised?

"You fucking double-crossed me," he said.

"How do you figure that? I'm here to talk about buying you out. I paid your past-due rent. I told you last night that I would pay you two thousand. I'll still pay you your two thousand minus the eight twenty-five past due rent, and I'll pay you one-fifty a week[2] for two months to teach me the business. After two months, you split."

Ramirez's expression changed a little, but the frown was still on his face.

"Kid, I told you two thousand plus the past due rent."

"You did, and I said no. You said you wanted two-fifty a week to stick around. I'm offering you one-fifty a week for two months."

I managed to say this with a straight face, though I had no idea where I would get enough to pay him, not to mention everything else. I had no idea how much the shop was making a week, if anything.

Ramirez read the lease.

"What did you do, fuck her?" His laugh was back.

"Get serious. She's a nice woman." I didn't mention what she said about him.

He put down the lease. I put it back in its envelope and hung on to it.

"Are you agreeable or not, Ramirez?"

"I'm fucked."

"I don't even know what I'm buying," I said. "I have no idea if you make a hundred a week or nothing. I know nothing."

I saw the whites of his eyes glisten when he laughed. It made me a little uneasy.

"I should get a toddy early," he said, getting up.

"If you do that, I'm going over to the meat market, then home. I'm not making any deals with you if there's a bottle between us."

He laughed.

We shook on the deal I had proposed. I would give him a deposit the following day of five hundred on the two thousand.

---

2. Adjusted for inflation, $150.00 in 1962 is equal to $1,284.87 in 2020.

He'd get more when I was satisfied that I had a complete picture of the business.

"Smarten up, kid," he said. "Who and what I owe is none of your business. You go downtown and get a city license under whatever name you are going to operate. You have the lease. You are coming in new and fresh, not assuming my headaches. If you don't believe me, go see a lawyer. There's a law office in every direction you drive on Brooklyn Avenue."

I didn't laugh aloud, but I was relieved I didn't have to pay anyone he owed. Why would I be liable for the debts of a former tenant?

"If a supplier comes over to complain about money owed, I'll tell them I only work here now. My business is gone. If they want to sue me, they can get in line. You leased the buildings and evicted me. You're clean as all hell," he said.

He laughed.

"I'm paying you money for the place. That's not an eviction, I'm sure."

"Give it to me in cash. You have control. You have a lease, kid."

I was silent, thinking. I got an hour's worth of information from him before the bottle came out.

"Bring my five hundred tomorrow," [3]he said. "And we can continue talking."

* * *

I had never been to the meat market next door. There were a handful of customers buying meat. A man wearing a wrap-around butcher's coat was behind the coolers. He smiled at me as I walked in. I'm sure he had no idea who the hell I was. I

---

3. Adjusted for inflation, $500.00 in 1962 is equal to $4,282.90 in 2020.

noticed another man in a wraparound apron carving meat on a big table. I took my place in line and looked around. They didn't just sell meat. Mexican food items were on display. In one corner was a counter with two big copper pots cooking something. A sign said they sold tacos and burritos. On weekends they sold tamales and menudo to go. You brought your own pot. They filled it with menudo.

I was finally next.

"Hi, my name is George Hatcher. Are you the owner, Jesse?"

"No, I'm Chris."

"Chris, here is a note from Mrs. Goldberg." I handed him a note on a small notepad.

Chris was surprised. He called Jesse over. I knew from Mrs. Goldberg that they were brothers, but other than them being good tenants, that's all I knew.

"Read this note from Goldberg," he said to Jesse.

Jesse was decades older than me but younger than Chris.

If Jesse was surprised by the note, he did not show it.

He handed it back to me, expressionless. "Come around the back," he said.

Chris stayed there and started working with the customer behind me in line.

"Is this a joke? Do you have a master lease? We have been trying to get a lease from her for years, and she says no leases."

"It's no joke. It's good for you because I'm willing to sublease to you for five years and maybe a five-year option."

He looked a little relieved and gestured toward a green-painted door that said, 'Employees only.'

"Let's go into the office and talk this through. We've been worried for years that something would happen to her, and we have no idea what her heirs will do with us."

Jesse was making it easier for me. I agreed to meet them the next morning at seven. They got in at six to start butchering the meat, and they opened at nine. I shook hands with Jesse and waved at Chris as I headed for the exit.

When I got home, I called Matt to get the scoop.

"I need another day or two," he said. I'm sorry you're missing these days."

"Don't worry about the pay. I can use a few days off."

I heard his grunt.

"Don't go getting lazy on me," he barked and was gone.

What would I tell Matt? I had to give him notice, and that was going to cost me. Now that the lease was signed, each day there was rent accumulating.

I was anxious. How would I swing the money I needed?

* * *

I called my friends across the way.

"I'm an anxious mess," I told Ava on the phone. "Either I need your services, or I'll have to settle for a massage from Cathy."

Ava giggled. "We are both free now and can come over, but I'll have to give Jaime your phone number in case he gets a client. Is that okay?"

"It's okay. You can answer the phone here."

"Okay, we'll be there."

"How is Jaime, as long as we're mentioning him?"

"His stitches are out. He's fine."

* * *

Chris unlocked the door to let me in the meat market at seven on the dot. Jesse called out from where he was cutting up meat.

"Good morning."

Chris, in pristine white, handed me a cup of black coffee. A seemingly endless supply of spotless aprons hung on a hook on the wall. I'd already learned their aprons were washed by a service that came several times a week. I sat on a stool, watching them carve up meat on a block. The shop had a distinctive smell, not just of raw meat but also spices. Two blocks were unused as we three were the only ones there.

"I am willing to sublease to you for five years with starting rent at seven hundred a month[4] for the first year, eight hundred for the third year, nine hundred for the fourth year, and twelve hundred for the fifth year. At that time, I will negotiate with

---

4. Adjusted for inflation, $700.00 in 1962 is equal to $5,996.06 in 2020.

Mrs. Goldberg and let you know my proposal to go on for another five years."

Chris's knife was as long as my arm. He moved it fast and sure on a carcass, slashing like some sort of grisly samurai. Jesse was making similar moves and was wearing some cool-looking goggles. Neither of their wrap-around aprons was as clean as they were a few minutes ago. Without missing a beat, he asked, "How much are you paying her?"

"I am making a profit for sure," I admitted, "but it's you that needs to decide if staying here warrants paying the rent, I just told you. I did the math last night. This is what I need. Plus, you are responsible for all repairs. Also, I need your agreement that I can build an office above your walk-in refrigerators backing up to the body shop."

"What you are asking is a big jump from the five hundred dollars we are presently paying," Jesse said.

"Come on. You have no lease. She told me you are solid-gold tenants and pay her right on time, and she has never had to come over here to collect the rent. I did not ask her to include your location on my lease. She decided that."

"What are you going to do with that asshole Ramirez?" Chris asked.

"He's a snake," Jesse said, turning his head to look at me in his bug-eyed alien-looking goggles.

"I'm going to let him stay and teach me the business, and then he's gone in three months."

"Ramirez is a jackass," Chris said.

I didn't ask why they felt that way about him.

"His creditors will shut you down," Jesse said.

"They can't do that. I'm a new owner with a lease. I got nothing to do with his past problems."

Chris said, "Son, get a lawyer."

"Thanks for the advice. Now talk to me about the sublease. Yes or no."

Jesse looked over to his brother and said, "The kid doesn't like conversation."

It was the first time they laughed.

"Tell us again how much rent you want and when you want it," Jesse said, putting down his knife and lifting up his goggles so I could see his eyes. One hand grasped the blade, the other rested on the block. I counted it a favorable sign that his arms weren't crossed over his chest.

I went over it again.

* * *

Two days later, Matt called me to say we were working the next day. I had finished negotiating with the brothers at the meat market. My next meeting would be after work. I told them I was giving notice.

One way or another, I would have to give two weeks' notice. I was on the freeway headed to the job we were doing in Arcadia as I tackled the problem of deciding whether to give notice to the manager at WESPAC - who hadn't seen me since he hired me to give my notice to Matt. Clear skies ahead.

I decided to tell Matt first. It was important to me. He'd been such an important figure in my life. I had the feeling that he cared about my future in this industry. The next two weeks, as we would work side by side, were going to be difficult. Maybe I was getting sentimental.

Matt was already on the roof of the bank building we were working on. I wasn't late. He was early. I went up the ladder. He was putting an elbow on a big copper pipe that he would tell me to weld.

"Matt got to talk to you. It's important."

His head was buried in pipe. He kept working.

"You going to get married again?"

He didn't look up at me. He was all about the pipe.

"Getting married would be easier than telling you this."

Matt stopped with the pipe. He straightened up and faced me. His hands were crossed over his chest. Not a good sign.

"What is it?" he asked, warily looking me over.

"How's the toe?" I asked.

"That's what you want to talk about?" he said skeptically. "Spit it out."

"I'm giving you two weeks' notice that I am quitting my job with WESPAC. I am going in another direction. I'm sorry."

"Tell me that again," he said.

He didn't yell. He didn't throw his glasses at me. He didn't punch me. He did snatch the hat off his own head, though.

"I'm going into business on my own. Not this type of business. I am giving you my two-week notice. You have been so good to me. I feel terrible about it."

He slammed his hat on the ground and got right up to my face. He pointed his finger at me like a weapon, but he didn't touch me.

"Hatcher fuck your notice! Get off my roof this minute. Now!"

"Matt, we're friends. Don't be like this."

His face turned five shades of red.

"Off my roof." His voice went up an octave, and I don't know how many decibels. It still wasn't a yell.

I backed away, and he was still moving toward me. I turned around and headed to the ladder. I felt bad. I had pushed his trigger.

I was about to get in my car, and something fell from the sky, narrowly missing me. I picked it up off the parking lot in two pieces. It was my lunch pail that had sailed off the roof.

"You forgot this, asshole!"

I looked up. There on the edge of the roof was Matt, scarlet-faced, shaking his fist at me. Even from the parking lot, I could see he was raving mad.

I got in my car and drove away, feeling lucky he hadn't chucked the pipe at me. I didn't go by WESPAC. I just went home, but when I got there, I called the manager.

He already knew.

"I'll mail your check," he said. "Good luck, George. Believe it or not, Matt will miss you, and our company will miss you."

* * *

I thought of staying home, but I still had to meet up with Jesse and Chris to get the sublease signed.

I told Ramirez everything was in limbo for two weeks, but I did give him the five hundred he expected.

* * *

I arrived much earlier than I had told them since I hadn't had to put in the day of work. The brothers already had their attorney draw up the sublease on my terms. They gave me a check for the first and last month's rent and the two-thousand-dollar deposit, a total of three thousand four hundred dollars[5] that I needed in the worst way. That gave me back what I had given Mrs. Goldberg, and I could use the balance towards the two thousand I had to give Ramirez. As long as I kept myself from thinking of Matt, I was a happy camper.

* * *

---

5. Adjusted for inflation, $3,400.00 in 1962 is equal to $29,123.72 in 2020.

The painter who had taken the dent out of my car and done a fabulous job of spot painting it was called Luis. He was from Mexico, twenty-seven years old, with a wife and son. He was one of the lucky ones who had a green card. Luis had been in Los Angeles for almost nine years, and his son was five, so I didn't ask if his wife was legal and assumed his son had been born in the USA. I sat at Ramirez's desk, and Luis sat across from me. The whole time, I was anticipating trashing the shabby office I was sitting in. It was the first thing a customer saw if they came in either entrance to the shop, and it was bad news.

"I don't know how I'm going to swing it yet, but I plan to do a revamp on the paint and bodywork sections and then expand other departments. I need to buy a spray booth and an oven. What else do we need to paint cars like the guy on TV that does them for twenty-nine ninety-five?"

"Jefe, that's a good idea. If you have the business with an oven, I can paint ten cars a day, including small repairs, dents, and all that. I have a friend who is a good body man. If I ask him to come over and work here when you're ready, and then I can concentrate on painting cars." His English was not perfect. His conversation was in Spanish and English.

I was getting excited.

"Who sells spray booths and ovens?"

"I can find out from the company that sells me my spray guns, the best on the market. My three spray guns are all DeVilbiss. They don't belong to Ramirez. The sales rep, I have his business card, I give to you or I call him. He does the rounds to all body shops and deals with the painters. He will know about spray booths and ovens."

"What else do I need for you to put out volume car painting?"

"Customers."

We laughed.

"What else?"

"Ramirez's compressor over there is shot. You need a moisture filter and new air hoses, not much more than that. We buy ready mix paint. I add a dryer so that in the oven, the paint dries fast."

"How fast?"

"Ovens are different. The people that sell them will tell you. They use heat lamps in an enclosure that covers the entire vehicle. I use a single heat lamp to spot dry when I'm in a hurry. I did it on your car because he promised it on a Sunday."

"It came out boss," I said for the fifth or sixth time.

"What made you want to do this and with Ramirez?"

"As long as I have people like you, I think this business and I will click. Ramirez is not my partner. He's going to teach me the biz."

"I don't want to say anything bad but be careful."

"I got it," I said.

At least everyone's opinion of Ramirez was consistent.

Before leaving, I talked to Ramirez again. He seemed happy I was taking over and didn't know about my worry about finding the money.

"You got anyone who sells spray booths?" I asked Ramirez.

"I know someone that buys used spray booths from folding shops then resells them with install included. I need to find his number tomorrow. I'll give it to you."

At five, like clockwork, the liquor bag showed up. Its appearance was not obvious, but now I knew what to look for. It stayed in the bag, probably so that I wouldn't bitch.

"What do you think a used one will run?"

"Maybe a thousand."

"Fuck, how much are they new?"

"Three times that or more."

"I see them on TV but never in real life."

"Go by Earl Scheib. They got them."

"I know," I said.

"It's just a twelve-foot-high box made of metal panels, twenty feet long and fifteen or so wide. The doors have filters in the front. Just folding doors and the filters are like air-conditioning filters. You should know about that." He laughed.

"I never got to install filters so large."

"Are you staying open while you clean up, or what?"

"I'll know soon," I said. "I need to find out where to buy the spray booth and oven before I talk to my bank. I believe those are the biggest items I need."

Ramirez filled his cup, smiling all the while. "You a smart kid," he said. He stood up, took one of his classic bows, and sat down again, laughing.

If I'd thought he was laughing at me, I'd have gotten pissed off, but he laughed all the time. And that bow of his.

* * *

I wasn't divorced yet, but both of us had already agreed. I can't remember if I told myself to forget marriage this time. But it was Friday night. I went home with thoughts of Olivia. My head was so full of business that I wasn't sure If I was to call Olivia or me. There was so much to take care of. If it hadn't been for the confrontation with Matt, it would have been a perfect business day.

Luis was going to be an asset. He had a Mexican electrician friend who worked as a laborer because he did not meet American licensing requirements. I asked Luis to find him. I had lots of electrical work that needed doing.

Matt was probably at home, cussing and complaining to his wife that I had let him down. If he hadn't chased me off, I'd have found a way to work two weeks and put the shop on pause. I never thought he'd order me off his roof. When I pictured him stomping his small round cap, it struck me as funny. I laughed from my parking spot all the way up the stairs, still laughing. I went straight to the shower, then put on a pair of shorts, a tee, and tennis shoes. I laughed, remembering my lunch pail flying off the roof and Matt standing there like the abominable snowman waving his fists at me.

I went to Shakey's again. I couldn't wait until Saturday to see Olivia. There was no host, so I walked through the crowd looking for a table. Olivia saw me, wowed me with her smile, and pointed out a two-seat table.

"I like your legs," she said.

"I like yours," I said.

"Are you ordering?"

"Eating for sure. Coke with lots of ice."

"I'll give it to you in a frosted beer mug."

"Love it," I said.

It was busy and getting busier. As I ate my favorite, a bowl of spaghetti and two meatballs, I saw Olivia working other tables. She brought me a fresh mug of coke and set a piece of paper next to it.

The manager watches all of us. If you want, I can come by after work if I can shower and use one of your shirts to lounge around in?

With the pen she left me, on the back of her note, I wrote my address.

* * *

At ten, I was in front of my building, waiting for her. I showed her my second parking spot.

She had a nice, well-cared-for VW van of indeterminable age. She got out of it with a backpack hanging off one shoulder and put her arms around me like we were old friends. I hugged her. We kissed.

I tried to help her with the backpack, but she was too fast for me, and I ended up holding her hand as we walked to my place. I opened the door to the building, and we went up the stairs to another door, holding hands.

"Nice apartment," she said. "How many TVs?"

"Two," I said.

"Dig it, lots," she said. "I smell like pizza. Can you point me to your shower?"

I showed her the bathroom in the bedroom I didn't use.

"Two bedrooms. You sell weed or something?"

She laughed and started undressing.

"I don't sell weed," I said. "I'll give you some privacy. Take your time. I put towels in the bathroom for you. You will love the water pressure."

"Hey, wait," she said, walking up to me, her uniform shirt unbuttoned. "I need to borrow a shirt for when I get out of the shower."

I walked to the closet and slid one side open.

"Take your pick," I said, "anything you want."

Her eyes got big as she took in the crammed-full closet.

"Damn, man, you got to be joshing. Thanks," she said.

We kissed. Her hand squeezed me through my shorts.

We smiled at each other. She was just as beautiful closeup, tired after her shift, and smelling like a deep-dish pepperoni and oregano pizza.

"I'm dying to check it out," she said.

I'm pretty sure she wasn't talking about the blue shirt she had draped over her arm.

I walked out and closed the door.

Olivia was perfect. What a score.

* * *

Now was when I thought about Sophia. I hoped she would hook up with someone who would make her happy. That would ease some of my guilt. In my highest moments of self-indulgent happiness, I felt guilty. I had a daughter, and where was daddy? Judy was a baby who didn't know any better. She wasn't missing Daddy. I know that I'm rationalizing, but isn't that real life? We are not perfect, and the story I tell today is different from the story I would have told then. I'm more experienced now. I lived the life.

If I'm going to write about myself, I have to tell it as it was.

I was a total jerk.

She came out of the bedroom in a blue polo shirt that fit me kind of baggy, the way I liked. It looked cute on her. She was a doll. As she walked towards me, the shirt almost hid that she had no panties on. Almost.

Olivia spent Friday night, Saturday, and Sunday with me. We went to McDonald's for breakfast, swam a little bit on Saturday, then on Sunday, I took her to the body shop and walked around the entire disaster area. Ramirez was there.

Ramirez smiled the whole time that Olivia was around. He gave me the phone number of a guy who bought and sold used spray booths and maybe ovens. The guy's name was Phil. I put the scrap of paper in my pocket and continued Olivia's tour of my soon-to-be model shop.

"I want you to see the before, so you'll be impressed by the after."

Olivia seemed ecstatic. It was like her whole body was an exclamation point.

"This place is huge. Are you sure you don't sell weed?"

"Hey, if you like weed, it's okay with me," I said. Maybe she was hinting.

"I don't do weed," she said.

She told me she didn't drink beer because it reminded her of the smell she took home from work every day.

I took her to Chinatown to my favorite restaurant. Now, most of the waiters smiled at me and knew my name. The booth where I normally sat was not in use, so they placed us there. I had brought Selena, and later Alicia, and probably Ava and Emma, before I brought Olivia. Everyone I know loved Chinese food. I wasn't much about taking leftovers home because I'm not much for leftovers, but that didn't stop me from ordering too much food.

After an early dinner, Olivia and I went to the pool. The weather was lovely, but it was fairly late, so no one else was around. We splashed quietly and floated around, having fun in the water. The girls saw us through their window. Dressed casually-shorts and crop tops-they came out and stood above us on the deck. They weren't in bathing suits, but at least they weren't dressed for dates.

"Join us," I said, waving hello.

Ava stood at the edge of the pool.

"I'm jealous," she said.

"I'm the jealous one in the family," Emma said.

"Eat your hearts out, ladies," Olivia said. "This weekend, he's all mine."

"Olivia, this is Emma and Ava. Ava and Emma, this is Olivia, queen of Shakey's."

"Not queen," Olivia laughed. "Princess, maybe. Or scullery maid."

Eva and Emma sat down with their feet in the water for a while, chattering away about nothing. Then Ava looked at her watch.

"We've got dates," she said to Olivia, "Or we'd give you a run for your money."

Imagining a night with the three of them was inevitable. It really spiked my libido. What if I had brought it up? I didn't think of it in time. But wouldn't that be lovely? Olivia didn't ask about what Ava and Emma did for a living, and I would never have told her. It was a boost to know that Olivia knew I had at least two neighbors who showed interest in me.

* * *

Next up was visiting the bank.

I went to see Mr. Holmberg, explained what I had done, and showed him the master lease and sublease. Now he wore a pair of thick, black bifocals. I'd known him since I was a boy, and he really hadn't changed at all. He'd never had a whole lot of hair, not as long as I'd known him. He just had a little more silver on the roof, but otherwise, he was unchanged, not only in his appearance but also in his enthusiasm.

He sat back in his chair with a big grin on his face and clapped his hands.

"You never cease to amaze me."

He had never put me down for the prison time. His total acceptance made him a superman to me.

We walked out of the bank together, and I drove us to the shop. On the way, I explained more.

"I got my car worked on there and never went inside. When I went back to get some more work done, I went inside for the first time. What I saw was this huge warehouse and, frankly, all the potential the shop wasn't living up to. It has everything. Location, size, talent. All it needs is polish. Believe me, it's rough." I stopped at a light and looked over at him. "It needs work. I know I bit off more than I should've, but once I got started, I couldn't stop to think. I just did it. I'm in the black, even after I pay Ramirez his fifteen-hundred-dollar balance. I have about a thousand, but that's not going to buy what I need."

"I'm impressed you're in the black," he said.

"Here goes nothing," I said, opening the accordion door for him.

He walked in and looked around, stepping his way through the same mess that had somehow inspired me to take a hundred-and-eighty-degree turn with my life.

"I'm junking the mess," I said. "The sublease put me over the top. The brothers are not going anywhere, and as long as they keep paying me, my rent is covered."

Holmberg stopped in the middle of the building and looked left and right, front and back, and upward. I could see him assessing the size of the building. I saw the grin on his face grow. We walked toward the desk where Ramirez was sitting, his paper bag thankfully not in sight. Holmberg kept grinning and walking alongside me.

I told Holmberg how Ramirez had taken in three small jobs and set the money aside for me. I had not counted the money.

"When you get this junk out," Holmberg said, "keep the store open. Every minute open, every job done, counts."

"I'm going to do that." I nodded.

Was he taking into account the crew I needed? I wished I could see his thoughts. I wanted him to see what a gold mine the meat market was for my situation, so we went to lunch next door and feasted on tacos. I told him about people coming in with their own pots and pans and filling them up with menudo. I introduced him to Jesse and Chris. They sat down with us for a few minutes. Holmberg asked lots of questions about their shop and bought some seasoning packets he said he would take home to his wife.

* * *

I could tell he appreciated the potential, and once we were back in his office, he had no shortage of advice.

"Our bank is stingy about capital loans for businesses that do not have a long track record. When we make those loans, they are credit lines to help the business with their accounts receivable or expand, not remodel. I *can* do equipment financing. Go shop for the equipment you need. Get a cost breakdown on everything. Bring it to me, and we'll go from there."

As I walked out of the bank, I was a bundle of joy. The day got a hundred shades brighter. I felt the weight of the world fall off my shoulders. All was right with the world. Nothing was set in stone, but I believed Holmberg would finance the big stuff I was worried about. I was able to put aside the stress until I could put it all on paper and figure out the overhead. Maybe people who buy a business normally do all of this in advance, but I had no choice but to jump in feet first without looking. Once I had a lock on getting the lease, I had to move as quickly as I did.

On my way back, I started looking for a lawyer on Brooklyn Avenue.

Ramirez had said there were plenty of them. I was going to stop at the first lawyer sign I saw, but there was no curb parking. I stopped at the second place. It was across the street from the direction I was driving. I parked and crossed the busy street without walking to the corner crosswalk.

I told the lady in reception that I needed legal advice for a new business. It was a small office in an older building. Everything was done in shades of brown: brown shag carpet, wood paneling. The receptionist was wearing a brown suit, though her skin was more on the green side like her summer tan was fading in the worst way. Or maybe she was part troll. It's hard to say. She said the meeting would cost me fifty dollars for thirty minutes. I paid in advance, not even knowing if this lawyer was any good. It took me five minutes to tell the lawyer, Carlos Navarro, that I held the master lease for the body shop two blocks away. I liked Navarro right away. He had warm brown eyes and a quick smile. His hair was a little on the long side, long enough that if Leonard had seen him, he'd have made one of his long-haired hippie jokes. All that I cared about was that he knew his stuff and didn't waste time getting things done.

"I want to name the shop Eastland Auto Center," I said. "What do I need to do?"

"I see you signed the lease personally, so you are on the hook personally."

"I don't understand?"

"Well, if you form a corporation and then sign a lease under the corporate name, you wouldn't have personal responsibility if the business goes bottom up. Fact is that you signed the lease personally, and now you're on the hook. You can file a fictitious name, a DBA that George Hatcher is doing business as Eastland Auto Center. A simple form, a small cost, and you are done. The other way, I file a corporation for you, which takes about a week, and you try not to buy or sign anything on a personal level, again, so you are not personally liable."

"I get it. The landlord would not have accepted a lease signed by a corporation. She'd want me on the hook for sure, so I did the right thing."

"Okay, do you want me to form a corporation for you under Eastland Auto Center?"

"How much?"

I spent another thirty minutes with him while he filled out a form. He needed to get approval for the name. I didn't understand the process yet. All in all, he figured it would take a week. I could wait.

"I will file for the name approval tomorrow. If I get the okay, and I probably will, the rest is very fast. The signs you want to put up, wait until I call you that the name has been approved by the State of California."

"That means I can't open a bank account or order business cards or stationary such as invoices until the name is cleared?"

"Correct. The same applies to phones. Anywhere you plan to use the corporate name."

"Carlos, my rent is running. Do it quick. I'll make you my lawyer from now on."

He grinned. "I can use the business."

His desk was cluttered with files. He looked busy to me.

"Let's talk about the debts Ramirez has," I said.

"Any debts Ramirez has are not your responsibility," Carlos said. "If anyone gives you a hard time, give them my card and tell them to call me."

We talked a little more; then I got up to go.

"I charge a fraction of what others charge," Carlos said. "I will keep track of anything you ask me to do after today, and you can come by and give me the cash when you have time."

"Deal," I said. "Carlos, I feel safe around you."

"It's self-serving for me to say, but it's good to have a lawyer take care of your affairs. Spend your time growing the business. Go get them."

We shook hands.

"George be careful with Ramirez. He has a bad reputation. I've never figured out how he lasted so many years there."

I nodded. "In three months, he's gone."

* * *

Luis not only got me an electrician, but he also found a sandblaster. The guy worked for a big company but could do the sandblasting work on the side over a weekend.

Mauro, the electrician, said I needed twenty-four-tube fluorescent fixtures that he would hang from chains on hooks from the high beams. The oval open ceiling sported six skylights. If it was painted, it could be beautiful.

I told Mauro I needed to wait until I could figure out how much it would cost to paint the ceiling.

"It will take two hundred gallons of paint, and everything would have to be out of here, and you will need some very tall scaffolds," he said. "With so many light fixtures up there, it will be daylight whenever you want it to be. No one will be looking at the ceiling above the lights."

I liked Mauro right away.

My need was not limited to fixtures, chains, bulbs, and hooks. I needed a new electrical panel. The existing one was a fire hazard. I didn't have enough breakers, and the electricity coming into the shop was six hundred amps.

"You can power up the block," Mauro said.

Mauro was willing to work for two dollars an hour.

"Once you finish the electrical work, I don't know what else I can use you for," I said honestly.

"I'll go back to the corner when I'm done," Mauro said. Like many other day workers, Mauro got labor jobs on the corner.

All the while, Ramirez was watching.

"How much we got in the drawer you been putting money in?"

"About two hundred."

"Good. I need cash to give Mauro."

Mauro figured two hundred would buy half the fixtures we needed, plus the electrical panel and breakers, wire, conduit, and too many things for me to remember.

"Two hundred will get us started on materials," he said. "How many hours a day you want me to work?"

"As many as you can," I said. "I want to light up this place.

Ramirez handed me two hundred [6] dollars from the drawer, where he said he had put all the money that had come in thus far on small jobs. I gave it to Mauro.

***

Ricardo, the sandblaster, was a short guy, chunky in the way that you could tell there was muscle there. I guess sandblasting is a full body work-out. He was not that much older than me, tan with long black hair worn in a ponytail tucked inside the back of his jumpsuit. He wanted fifty dollars to buy silica sand to do the job. He showed up in a crisp white canvas paint-spattered jumpsuit. At first, he wanted two hundred for sandblasting the entire outside of the building except for the meat market. I left him in my embarrassingly bad office as I went next door to confer.

Jesse and Chris freed up three minutes, leaving their shop in the hands of their weekend backup guy, who I'd never met before. They poured me some of their very good coffee, and we sat in their office.

"I'm sandblasting the outside of body shop this weekend. Then I'm going to patch up any holes that might surface, then paint. You don't have to do it, but I got the guy in the shop waiting to see if you want in or not. No pressure. If you don't want in, I'll just do my part of the building."

"How much?" Jesse asked.

Chris said, "Jess, we don't need it."

"Four hundred for the sandblasting. The finish and paint are another story. Plus, we need to agree on the paint. We can't have two different colors on the exterior."

Chris was moaning, but he understood.

"How much are you paying to sandblast?" Chris asked.

---

6. $226 in 1963 is same as $1,910 in 2020

"All you need to know is that four hundred dollars will clean up your walls, and you'll be glad you did it. I have a great electrician putting up a bunch of light fixtures and handling some rewiring for me. If you need electrical work, just raise your hand."

Chris said, "We do have electrical work we need. Let's see how he does with you."

"Agreed," I said. "What's the verdict on the sandblasting? Are you in or not?"

"It's going to be a mess," Jesse said. "That sand will be everywhere."

"While it's going on, have your customers park across the street at Safeway. There are over two hundred parking spots there."

I went back to my shop. Ramirez had gone off somewhere, which was okay because it gave me privacy to talk to Ricardo. He was very accommodating.

"My boss would charge eight hundred dollars. I'll do the whole building for three hundred [7]starting early Saturday and finishing on Sunday. That includes the silica and rental of the compressor I need."

We shook hands on it. I gave him a hundred out of my pocket.

"I owe you two hundred on Sunday," I said. "And don't discuss how much I'm paying you."

He grinned. "It's nobody business but you and me," he said in Spanish.

Paying Ricardo left me twenty dollars and change until I could go to the bank.

* * *

---

7. Adjusted for inflation, $300.00 in 1962 is equal to $2,569.74 in 2020.

Ramirez came back ten seconds after the money exchange. He was carrying some fast-food bags and offered me one. I declined.

He sat down at the desk and unwrapped a hamburger.

"How much you charging the meat market?"

"They are paying a fair price," I said. "Why you being nosey?"

"It is none of my business," Ramirez said with a laugh. I noticed he dropped one of the paper bags in a desk drawer. I had a pretty good idea of what was in there, and it wasn't food.

* * *

I called my mom to let her know that I was going into business for myself. Maybe I should have done it in person, but I was apprehensive about her reaction and was prepared to defend myself. I felt sure she would want me to stick with the heating and air career path, especially after I had worn their ears out boasting so much to her and my dad Leonard about that job. I thought she would give me a bad time about quitting. They both still worked jobs for other people and seemed okay with it.

"I guess being my own boss is in my blood," I said. "One weekend, I'll bring you over to see it," I said.

"When you have time," she said. "What are you using for money?"

"I saved some money," I said.

"Leonard has some money," she said.

I ended up borrowing three thousand dollars[8] from my parents. I'd had no idea they had that kind of money stashed. According to my mother, most of it was from little bonuses the tenants at the building gave my dad, plus money I had given her. Inevitably, I remembered the money I had borrowed from

---

8. Adjusted for inflation, $3,000.00 in 1962 is equal to $25,697.40 in 2020.

Thelma that went to the rotten-thieving lawyer in Mexico. I suppose they didn't have any money then. That was years back.

I promised repayment at every opportunity, but they waved me off and told me there was no pressure, and they both said they'd wait to see the shop when it was fixed up.

* * *

The biggest impact so far was the deal with Hollenbeck Towing. I gave the driver some money, and he made trips back and forth to the junkyard, where he hauled all the abandoned cars to be crushed. Ramirez claimed ownership though he had pink slips for only two. Without the trashed vehicles filling up the place, the shop seemed twice as big.

Mauro put in the electrical panel and started running the conduit. In the daytime, with skylights, it was amazing how much room there was. I took to wearing jeans and a white t-shirt as my uniform. Maybe some people thought I kept wearing the same clothes, but I had a lot of jeans and a whole bunch of T-shirts. The greasy floors messed up pair after pair of white tennis shoes.

I looked at pictures the used spray booth guy had in stock. They were just a pile of dirty metal with dry paint in all colors. I told him I had the financing and preferred buying new equipment. He gave me the name of a company that sold new spray booths and another company that sold the ovens. I gave him fifty bucks for the valuable information. I couldn't find anything even close in the Yellow Pages, and that's all we had then.

Holmberg advanced two thousand for the spray booth[9] after

---

9. Adjusted for inflation, $1,000.00 in 1962 is equal to $8,565.80 in 2020.

it was installed and seventeen hundred [10] for the bake oven. Mauro ran power for a whole herd of heat lamps.

Luis was anxious to get the paint department going. He brought me temporary help to speed the process, an unemployed couple who were janitors. He found them on the street corner looking for day work.

It took the couple two full days of vigorous, non-stop scrubbing and teamwork to clear the cement floor and walls of grease and grime that had been there since dinosaurs roamed the earth.

Mauro was a great runner for me. He rented a twenty-foot extension ladder similar to the ones I climbed up and down working with Matt. The couple went up to the roof, cleaned the filthy skylights from the outside, then used the same ladder indoors, using cross beams for support and cleaning the interior. Then there was light. All that light highlighted how much the ceiling needed painting, but it was not practical. This was an auto center, not a hospital.

Day laboring carpenters built a pretty big office on top of the walk-in refrigerators. Ramirez's old office was converted into a small waiting area for customers. I ordered a soda vending machine from Coca-Cola so we could all get refreshments when we were thirsty. Besides the waiting area, I had a small office with open doorways installed. For now, Ramirez was using it.

When a customer needed an estimate, I went out there with Ramirez. The cost of car parts was listed in the Mitchell book, the estimate writer's bible. It was a monthly subscription that was constantly updated with the latest cars and price changes. The prices weren't always correct. Often, finding a part took a phone call to the dealer. Dealers wanted the business and gave good and rapid service.

It was the Mitchell book that helped me learn parts termi-

---

10. Adjusted for inflation, $1,700.00 in 1962 is equal to $14,561.86 in 2020.

nology. Turret, cowl, rocker panel, fenders, undercarriage. I could go on and on. When writing an estimate, especially for an insurance company, you need to name the part you repair or replace. The term used so many times it got scribed into my brain right away was R and R, meaning Remove and Replace.

A sign company installed metal signs on both sides of the building. It was a groundbreaking moment for me when I went outside and saw the sign marking my shop as my Eastland Auto Center, sitting there on top of that newly painted wall space. Metal signs were my advertising strategy. Paint your car in one day: thirty-five dollars, baked enamel.

I wanted to push painting at first. Thirty-five dollars was cheap, and if the customer came in with a dent or something, so much the better, and I was counting on that.

I hired a bodyman so Luis could concentrate on painting. My hunch was that we would have a lot of paintwork. I made a deal with the bodyman that he would get forty percent of what we charged the customer for bodywork. That way, I wouldn't get snowed under with payroll. I warned him it might be slow at first and that it was okay for him to moonlight with other shops.

After the lights were installed, Ramirez and I went across the street to the Safeway parking lot to look at the shop from there. It looked fantastic! I had sandblasted walls, fresh paint, new signs, oven lights, and overhead lights. It was all marvelous. It looked so marvelous that I went to the meat market and dragged Chris and Jesse across the street to look. Their signs were up, and while their side looked like a meat market, it blended with my side of the building.

* * *

I made enough money from the signs, electrical, and other things they needed from my workers to pay for the work I had done on my side.

Jesse told me, "We have a brother who's a general contractor. We don't call him because he charges us more than he charges strangers. I know you are making money on us, but Chris and I know we are getting a good deal."

"Jesse, Peace."

Jesse put his arm around me. I gave him the peace sign, a big thing going around at the time. A couple of decades earlier, the same sign was V for victory. I got tight with Jesse and Chris. Chris was the serious one, but we all took to each other. It got to the point that when I walked in, Chris would ask, "How much is it going to cost us this time?"

Jesse was a good-looking guy and had a great laugh. He was married, but I was sure some of his women customers came to the store in order to see him. He always had one of those butcher jackets and, underneath, a white shirt and tie. Imagine butchering meat wearing a tie under a butcher's apron. Every time I pointed it out, I got that laugh from him.

Chris said, "Put on a jacket. We'll teach you the meat business."

"It will cost you. No free here," Jesse said.

When he finished my electrical work, I gave Mauro some extra money, and then we spent an hour at the meat market making a list of the things that the brothers needed to have done, like high voltage work on their freezer and walk-ins.

I made a deal with Mauro that we'd split the profit after parts and his labor at two dollars an hour. I made over five hundred dollars for my end. I was elated and Mauro was like the happiest guy on earth.

"Your electrician is a real electrician," Chris said one day. "I had him wrong."

Maybe I should become a contractor. All along, I had the money in the bank that I owed Ramirez. Before officially opening, I paid him off.

"Starting next week, I'll pay you the weekly for staying on for three months."

"I been here six weeks."

"Doesn't count. We're not officially open."

Outfitted in three changes of white pants and white shirts, brand new from a uniform company, Ramirez looked nothing like the greasy, grungy spark plug he'd been when I first met him. His name was embroidered as he liked. Like a new man, he sat behind his new desk, leaning back in the new chair I bought him. He hardly looked like the same person without his raunchy old coveralls that looked like he painted and slept in them.

I bought myself a desk and some other furniture for my office upstairs. I had a vantage point from up high with louvered windows I could open and yell through to get someone's attention. When the phone company installed phones in my office, Ramirez's office, and on the shop floor, I had a public address system installed. I could press a button on any phone and broadcast through two speakers the phone man installed. We were moving up in the world.

When I mailed Mrs. Goldberg the first rent check, the building was lit up like Christmas. From the Brooklyn side of the street, a person passing by would have to turn and look at the big building and the glare of the bake oven with its many heat lamps.

Luis had all new hoses to connect his spray guns and the sander. The big, new compressor that ran air for the paint department would also provide air wherever it was needed. The compressor was twice the size that Luis needed, but after I learned how air is used in a shop, I knew a five-gallon would never be enough. It didn't matter what the salespeople wanted to sell me. I let them pitch so I could learn. The new compressor was a thing of beauty, especially when I remembered how the old one had looked. I sometimes found myself polishing it off if dust or fingerprints got on it.

Chapter 13
Grand Opening

The day I officially opened, the market owners and I put banners above the parking lot to draw the attention of the passing traffic and the shoppers at Safeway Market.

We had been open since I made my deal with Ramirez but not officially. On the day we were officially open, it was a Monday.

"If it works with painting, I'll expand to mechanical or some other department," I told Ramirez. "You can talk me into other departments later, but not now. I'm keeping the overhead low."

I remembered the grand opening of the ice cream parlor in Juarez.

I had a small crew: Luis, the painter; Felipe, the bodyman; Emily, the masker. I needed more help than that, but it was easy to find tradesmen like mechanics, upholsterers, etc. I had explored a number of trades. Thanks to Ramirez, my eyes were wide open to expand to more than painting. My team agreed that if we didn't have customers coming in, they would keep busy tidying up or practicing for a wave of jobs. My masker,

Emily, told me she could mask one car per hour, depending on the size. A sedan would take an hour. At Luis's suggestion, I had purchased two masking stations on wheels with rolled paper, cutter, and masking tape.

Felipe, my bodyman, said he would help sand cars if he wasn't doing a job. Luis said he'd put Emily to sand if necessary. Sander was a position I would have to fill sooner rather than later. It depended.

In the waiting room were twelve paint colors we offered on the thirty-five-dollar paint job. The colors were displayed on metal samples fixed to one of the walls, visible from nearly all over the shop.

My uniform was still jeans, a T-shirt, and tennis shoes. No one would guess I was the boss. It felt good.

When meat market customers peeked in the shop, Ramirez would hand them a card and ask them if they wanted a paint job for thirty-five dollars and get their car back the same day or in a couple of hours if in a big hurry.

Monday morning, I stood at the Brooklyn Avenue entrance facing the parking lot and Safeway across the street. An hour after we opened, a white VW drove up. Ten minutes later, the lady was picking her paint and signing the invoice. Luis drove the car in and started water-sanding it.

The lady asked Ramirez how much it would be to fix the little dent on the rear right fender. Ramirez charged her fifteen dollars. It was Felipe's first bodywork, and when he was done, it looked like new. Jesse loaned me a 35m camera, and I took lots of pictures of the VW masked, then in the spray booth, fifteen minutes later, in the oven. It was dry in twenty minutes, but Luis left it there for thirty minutes.

I touched the paint. It was dry. The owner of the car came out of the waiting room and gasped with glee when she saw her blue car.

"I can't believe it," she said.

Ramirez walked her over to the car.

She touched it as I had.

"I thought it was a scam. It's not a scam. I will send you many of my friends."

Emily removed the tape and paper like an absolute pro. The final touch was cleaning the windshield. It was all so fast. It was wonderful.

We painted seven cars that day. Afterward, Ramirez and I were alone, both checking out how the day had gone.

I was giddy, drunk with success. I was tempted to have a celebratory drink with Ramirez, but I didn't crack. The deal I made with him was that if he was going to drink, it had to be after six, and both entrances had to be closed, so it was closed for everyone outside. I didn't want anyone to see him drinking or smell the liquor on him. I stopped before banning his paper bag altogether. I didn't have the heart to take that away from him, too.

Once the doors were closed, Ramirez walked around the empty shop carrying that tiny paper cup he liked to use. I watched him from my office above. With the frosted louver windows closed, nothing could be seen from the shop floor. If the louver windows were open, a different story. Mostly I kept them open.

* * *

My painter brought in a sander, Manuel, who also did masking when it was needed. If I could do volume and keep my overhead down, I would stay in the black. My painter was getting more than twice the minimum wage, with the understanding that there was no overtime. So, he made sixteen dollars[1] a day. My bodyman rejected the percentage deal I had offered him and wanted sixteen dollars a day like the painter. It was less risky for me if he was on percentage, but I rolled with what he wanted. My masker Emily was happy with her dollar fifty an hour, with the agreement she would get paid for as many hours as she worked but not overtime. Ramirez said she probably made a buck an hour at her last job, and I should have done the same, but last year, the minimum wage went up to a dollar twenty-five. My sander and backup masker agreed to work for twelve dollars a day. He asked for that. The hundred fifty a week I paid Ramirez was like tuition for me. I was learning fast. Ramirez was a good teacher, and I didn't feel like he was holding back.

On the second day, customers were inquiring about the paint. Both Ramirez and I were asking if they had bodywork that needed to be done. I looked to Ramirez for bodywork pricing or called over my bodyman to say how much time was involved. So far, none of the bodywork had required replacing parts.

Dents like the one I had on the door are pulled out. A top-notch job would be to remove the door panel from the inside and pound out the metal. No matter the method, the job ended up with *Bondo* filler. Bondo is a fast-drying putty. The bodyman grinds the dry Bondo, then sands it so smooth that it is invisible once it is painted. I'm making it sound simple, and though it technically is, doing it well is an art. You have to know how to use it. Luis, who took care of the dent on my Impala, walked me through the process.

We painted nine cars that second day, four of them with small dings and scratches that required extra for the bodywork. Everyone worked ten hours to finish those nine cars. Not everyone waited for the car either. Some were next-day pick-ups.

---

1. Adjusted for inflation, $16.00 in 1962 is equal to $137.05 in 2020.

Jesse had told Mrs. Goldberg how amazing the first two days had been. On Wednesday, she appeared in her old limo.

"What a surprise," I said. "It's great to see you."

I hugged her, then shook Lionel's hand.

"Oh my. Look at all the lights," she said. "Show me what you've done."

I started walking her around, pointing out the sand-blasted, patched, painted exterior, all the new wiring, the new waiting area, the cleaned-up skylights, the walk-thru office, pointed to the office up the stairs, the new furniture, the PA system, the paint booth, the paint oven, the big compressor, the masking stations, and the staff. Before we got through everything, she saw Ramirez come inside after talking to a customer.

She stopped dead in her tracks. "What's he doing here?"

She lifted up her cane and pointed it at Ramirez like she had him in the sights of a locked and loaded double-barrel shotgun.

"He's staying three months to teach me what I don't know about the business," I said.

"Keep an eye on him. He's no good," she said in a loud whisper that was probably heard in the parking lot.

I actually felt bad for Ramirez. It didn't matter that he wasn't being told what I was told. Everyone had the same opinion of him.

"Mrs. Goldberg, I can have your car painted and finished in three hours."

She didn't take me up on it.

"You're a fine young man," she said, touching my face.

I had shown her everything except the office above the refrigerators. She didn't want to tackle the stairs. She was all smiles throughout the tour, then watched a car being dried in the oven while another car was being masked in preparation for the spray booth. She watched a dented fender being brought back to perfection.

Jesse came over from the market to say hello to Mrs. Goldberg and shook her hand. I could see she liked him. When he left, Chris came to see her.

She talked to me about him but never said a word to Ramirez or acknowledged his existence. It was like he was invisible.

* * *

The third day was as successful as the days before. Before everyone went home, everything was put in its place. The paint department had a morning and evening checklist. The body department had a morning and evening checklist. Ramirez had never had anything like that, but we'd had something like that at the ice cream parlor for the side work. Matt had something from the construction crews he'd called a punch list and milestones to get a job done. Before the official opening, when days were slow, we had just tailored those lists to fit the day-to-day so that all the equipment new to us stayed as new as possible for as long as possible.

After everyone had gone, Ramirez had his cup out and brought up Mrs. Goldberg.

"I do not understand how you won that old bag over like you did. Jesse and Chris have been tenants for years, pay their rent on time, she likes them, and even they couldn't get a lease out of her."

"Ramirez, don't call her an old bag. I don't like it."

He didn't apologize or take it back; he just raised his eyebrows, flashed that charming grin did his signature bow, and walked to his new office.

* * *

Ramirez was on me to drive over to Atlantic Boulevard, where the streets were paved with used and new car dealers. I bought my Impala from the Chevrolet dealer there.

"We can get tons of paintwork," Ramirez said.

"I'm going to do it. For now, we are maxed out."

Ramirez laughed. It was a laugh I couldn't read.

* * *

I painted my lawyer's car for thirty-five dollars, but he got a fifty-dollar paint job. Carlos, my lawyer, wanted a lavender, one of the enamels that cost fifty. All paint jobs had a two-year guarantee for peeling or fading.

Carlos asked me, "Why only two years on the warranty?"

"Because we're legit. If your paint peels on its own or fades, you bring it back, and we repaint it for fifteen dollars."

"Is that because I'm your lawyer?" Carlos laughed.

"Nope. Standard warranty goes for everybody."

"I like that guarantee."

One after another of our customers said the same thing about our guarantee.

"That's not all. If you hate the color once you drive off, we'll repaint it in another color for $15 dollars. The catch is that you can't have a one-day service. It takes two days."

I invented the guarantee. At fifteen dollars, it was close to being my cost. I didn't know for sure, but I figured that would cover it all. No loss. The person who loved the guarantee was my banker. My attorney worded it out and brought me a rubber stamp to put it on the invoice.

"A very honest guarantee," Carlos said.

* * *

Finally, I spent several hours a day visiting used car dealers along Atlantic Boulevard. Within days my visits began to pay off. One car dealer said, "Why should I pay five bucks extra? Scheib charges twenty-nine bucks."

"You got to be curious."

I handed him a fold-out, a simple color brochure with a picture of the shop from the outside, the spray booth, the oven, and the basic colors we offered at that price. I didn't talk to a car dealer who didn't compliment the look of the shop that was depicted in the brochure.

And the guarantee.

"I'll send you a car or two and see how you do."

That was what they said, but I didn't press. We were busy.

Every used car dealer I spoke to wanted to know if I had an upholstery department.

"Upholstery is coming," I promised. I wasn't in a hurry, for now.

Every car dealer I talked to asked if Ramirez had anything to do with the shop. I told them he was employed for three months, then he was out. I was in charge.

There was a lot going on in owning a business. Carlos hooked me up with an insurance agent that sold me liability insurance and workers' compensation insurance. I had insurance on my car, but I never gave business insurance any thought. When Ramirez found out I got a policy, he said it was crazy to pay for those things.

My attorney said I needed to put at least half of my workers on the payroll. I only had five.

"You have workers' compensation insurance but no employees," Carlos said.

"Wrong. As soon as I have people on payroll and know the monthly payroll, the agent will activate the workers' compensation insurance in case a worker gets injured."

"George, if a worker gets hurt, you are on the hook."

I knew that much, but I also knew that my painter, masker, sander, and bodyman wanted to get paid in cash. Two of them didn't have a green card. I needed to mull that over. Jesse and Chris at the market told me that if I had payroll, I'd have employer contributions to pay the Internal Revenue Service and other government agencies. That was enough to put off setting up payroll.

I was getting good at writing estimates for bigger jobs. I had been through the Mitchell Book so much that I knew exactly where to go for what we needed. I had all the dealers' part department phones and four junkyards where I could buy used parts if the customer didn't want to spring for new.

I never before realized that junkyards are big business.

As much as I didn't want to do it, I had to hire another bodyman. There was no way to get the work out without a full crew. I paid him a flat daily fee and stopped offering a piece of the job. No one wanted to roll the dice on business being good, even though the shop was buzzing.

The phone rang off the hook. People drove by on the way home or to work, then called and wanted to know about getting their car painted.

We asked them to come in.

"I may need a secretary," I told Ramirez.

He laughed.

"I had one, then two for a long time. Those were the days."

He laughed again, a dirty laugh. I could tell his secretaries were doing way more for him than just typing.

"I got plenty of pussy going on after work," I said. "I'm thinking of someone who can answer the phone and file the work we're putting out. Carlos got us a resale number with the State Board of Equalization. A report is due every thirty days to pay the sales tax collected from all the jobs."

Ramirez said, "Ask the customer to pay cash. No deposit at the bank. Nothing to report."

"Have I ever told you about how I did over two years up in Tracy?"

"What is that?"

"Prison," I said.

"Oh, bullshit," he said. "You ain't old enough to have spent two years in prison."

I didn't need to convince him. I knew it was true. I gave him a look and said, "I'm paying taxes."

Ramirez laughed and walked away.

* * *

I always went to see Jesse and Chris before they were open for business to have coffee with them and shoot the breeze. After Ramirez laughed me off, I started to tell Jesse and Chris about my experience of being locked up one morning. They didn't bite either. They both laughed and didn't even look up from the meat they were cutting up.

* * *

I saw Olivia from Shakey's regularly. At no charge, I painted her VW ivory, close to the original. If we were really horny, she'd come over after work, worried she would smell like pizza and beer. She always showered before we got down after her work. We also saw each other some weekends. Friday night through Sunday. Olivia never pushed to be together. She was solid, and I loved her and her casual attitude. We weren't romantic, not like we were that kind of couple. We were best fucking friends.

Olivia claimed she wasn't seeing anyone, but our understanding was that she could see anyone she wanted, and I could see anyone I wanted. I did see other ladies, and she knew it. We didn't sit around chattering to each other about our extra-curricular activities, but we both knew the score.

I also loved Ava and Emma, my working girls. I painted their car, too, at no charge. After that, they refused to charge me for sex. If I was home and not with Olivia and one or both were free, I'd get a visit. They dropped in and hung out, sometimes would fool around, sometimes not.

On the home front, I was still married to Sophia. Neither one of us was pushing to rush the divorce, but we were in agreement that we were getting a divorce.

Some days I did go see my daughter after work. Not often enough. I would take her a gift and kiss my soon-to-be ex-wife on the cheek. Sometimes I even had dinner with them, but it wasn't just us at the table. The grandparents were always in attendance except when we escaped to the master bedroom and had fast sex. Sophia had no problem with that but was adamant I couldn't move back in unless I gave up my apartment.

I paid the rent and expenses for the house they were living in and never complained. It was only right I take care of anything my wife and daughter needed, even the weight of having the grandparents at the house full time. It wasn't like they didn't have an apartment, a nice apartment it was nicely furnished and spacious.

I heard, but don't recall how I heard that Sophia had an old boyfriend hanging around her, but I didn't ask her about it. I wished it was true.

In the early morning, Ramirez and I were busy, busy. We didn't take appointments, but people who came in to talk about a paint job returned, and when they did, it was usually in the morning because most people wanted the one-day service.

Chapter 14
Elena

I was talking to a customer that was dropping off her car. I looked up and walking across the parking lot headed in my direction was the hottest lady, ever. The smiling girl walking towards me was a clone of Christine. Same incredible shape, same perfectly lovely face. She stopped ten feet from the customer's car, waiting for me to finish, still smiling. The customer left, Luis took the car, and I turned to the lovely brunette with a fabulous body in a tiny short skirt, white flats, and a white blouse with collar opened, revealing more cleavage than it covered. Her hair was blacker than brown, glossy, and moved with her.

"How can I help you?" I asked.

She extended her hand, and I did the same. We shook hands. Her fingernails were long and beautiful, like the hand of a model or something.

"My name is Elena," she said. "I'm looking for a job."

"My name is George," I said.

"I know. My aunt had her car painted here a couple of days ago. She described you pretty well. She said you were wearing a t-shirt and jeans, and you own the place."

A couple of yards to my left, Ramirez was taking care of a customer.

Elena waved at him

"Hi."

"You know Ramirez?" I asked.

"I dated his son for a while."

Surprising. "I didn't know he had a son," I said. Outside of these walls, I really didn't know anything about Ramirez. He never talked about family. "I think you are too classy to work here. My office is upstairs. Let's talk."

I pointed in the direction of the stairs to my office.

"Classy or not, I can be whatever it takes," she said as we walked. "I'll wear a uniform."

I didn't do it intentionally, but I pointed, and she went first. I was behind that fabulous body. Hey, I was twenty-one. By the time we entered my office, I was stiff as a bat.

Elena had a lovely face and a killer physique. I can't describe her walking up the stairs without getting ex-rated, and I'm pretty sure on her part it wasn't on purpose.

No one had ever sat on the leather couch up there until she sat on it. I seldom used my office because I worked downstairs. Elena sat on the sofa. I sat behind my desk to hide the bulge in my jeans.

"Are you hiring?" Elena asked, crossing her legs.

I shuffled papers on my desk and looked down at them to keep from staring at her, sitting there like a ripe peach. "I need someone to file job invoices. More importantly, I need someone to keep track of the sales tax we charge for each job so I can report it."

"Don't you have an accountant?"

"No accountant yet, but I have a lawyer and an insurance agent so far."

"As busy as you are, it's probably a good idea to have an accountant. He will add up the sales tax on each invoice, fill out a form, and tell you how much to pay the State Board of Equalization," she said.

Her knowledge impressed me already. "Elena, you must be an accountant."

"Nope. Not an accountant."

"I need someone to answer the phones, but that's boring."

"I've answered phones before," she said.

She looked straight at me. I could have fallen into those big brown eyes.

"I'll be honest with you. If I hire you, I'll be distracted. You're beautiful."

The room got so quiet the distant whoosh of the spray booth exhaust seemed louder than usual. I could hear the grinder going. Maybe I shouldn't have paid her a compliment. She hadn't responded yet.

"Are you married?" I asked.

She shook her head. Her dazzling smile was still there. Every girl I'd fallen for had a mesmerizing smile. Her lips were glossy red, fresh like she'd bitten into an apple or a cherry snow cone, and the color had stayed on her lips.

She got up. I should say I watched her get up. She moved beautifully.

"Are you doing anything tonight?" she asked.

I said, "You tell me."

"We can discuss the job and pay," she said. "Drive South on Rowan, left side of the street, the third house after Safeway."

"You live close," I said.

"If you don't pick me up at eight, I'll understand," she said. "It was nice meeting you."

"Just like that?" I stood behind my desk. It still wasn't polite for me to come out yet.

"To be continued," she said. "All you need to do is come by for me."

It struck me like something Marilyn Monroe would say - only Marilyn was a blonde.

As she went down the stairs, I heard whistles. I opened one of the louvered windows to yell out but stopped myself. I had the PA system. And what the fuck, fuck it. She probably loved the attention.

* * *

After she was gone, I asked Ramirez, "What do you know about Elena? She's looking for a job."

He laughed. "The Girl is red hot. My son David and she were seeing each other regularly, and then it went south—like everything snapped."

"She lives down the street," I said.

"Yeah, her aunt painted her car here a few days ago. You took care of her."

"She mentioned something about it."

"She lives in one of those big homes. I have never been inside. It is a vintage house. It is older than me. She lives with her mother's sister, the aunt who was here. Her Mom died or something. I don't know about the dad. I have never heard about him. Her mother owned two mortuaries. Her aunt operates them now."

"Mortuaries?"

"Dead people. You know. Like, dead. Big business."

I felt shocked, grossed out, and a little intrigued.

Ramirez laughed at my response.

* * *

I was busy until seven-thirty when a customer picked her car up. Ramirez was complaining that he needed to buy his bottle. I wondered if he was getting booze withdrawals. It was way past five.

There was no way around it. I needed more help. We were painting ten cars daily. Half of them got about thirty- or forty dollars' worth of bodywork, giving me an average of sixty dollars per car-six hundred dollars[1] a day, plus.

* * *

I had not forgotten I was still married. I wanted to believe my wife had a boyfriend who loved her and made her as happy as she deserved to be. If she did, I didn't need to feel so guilty. I was a prick. I wanted to believe that I became that way after my first and second marriages failed, and now my third marriage was also a failure. The occasional sex I had with Sophia when I went over to see Judy was infrequent. It had tapered away. I suspected there was a boyfriend who was taking care of what I failed to do. She brought it up the last time I was there when we had just started our sex encounter, and I had just kissed her.

"Give up your apartment and come home," she said. Why do you need more than me?"

I kissed her. "Don't blame yourself," I said. "It's me. You're too good for me."

"You sound like a con man," she said. "Fuck me already and split."

* * *

I went straight from the shop to Elena's house. Elena was standing between cars parked along the curb. I made a U-turn in the middle of the street to get to her side. It's a good thing there was no streetcar to run into. She waved. I stopped and reached across to open the door, but she beat me to it.

---

1. Adjusted for inflation, $600.00 in 1962 is equal to $5,139.48 in 2020.

"Right on time," she said in her musical voice. Did I have it bad or what? Her voice hit my ear like a melody.

"Always," I said. "Sorry, I didn't change. I just closed up."

"You look so cute today. I'm glad you have the same clothes on."

In the driver's seat, I turned to face her. In the dark, I couldn't tell yet if she had on shorts or a skirt, but her upper thighs gleamed. She leaned my way, and I leaned her way, the console between us like the continental divide. Our lips tapped. Her fragrance was a turn-on. I strongly remembered Christine, but this was Elena, not a girl from my past.

"Are you hungry?"

"Fucking starved," she said.

"I'll take you wherever you want to go."

"I'm good with food to go. Let's hit a motel, and we can eat there."

I laughed at her - reminding me again of Christine.

"I'll laugh if you tell me what's so funny," she said, reaching for and expertly finding my growing member.

I thought it better not to mention Christine. "How about The Hat?"

"Love that place," she said.

"I have an apartment close by. It's better than a motel."

In the light of the restaurant parking lot, I saw she was wearing shorts and an untucked t-shirt that revealed her nipples. No way was she wearing a bra.

We got out to order and ate our pastrami on the patio. She sat across from me. Her hair was so different. It moved and caught the light and framed her face. Earlier at the shop, she was not combed this way. She was hot!

"I feel like we've done this before," I said. I bit into the warm bread. The mustard was just perky and salty enough to make the pastrami hit all the notes my tongue could taste. She reached across the redwood table and dabbed something from the corner of my mouth. I pulled a napkin from the holder on the table, dabbed the corner of hers, and got a touch of lipstick on the napkin.

"Maybe we did in another life."

I remembered her aunt operated mortuaries that Elena's mom once owned. I wondered why she didn't work at her family business.

* * *

We entered my apartment from the parking area. When we walked in, the first thing she said was, "You live alone?"

"I do."

"I've never seen such an orderly, clean bachelor pad."

I was going to give credit to the Navy and prison, but I just smiled and didn't even say thanks.

Elena was not bashful. She checked out the entire apartment while I got us a beer.

"I have cold mugs in the freezer," I said.

"I'll drink it too fast from a mug," she said.

We sat on the sofa, clicked our Coors cans, and took a drink. She set her can down on the coffee table, took my can, and put it next to hers. Her arm went over my right shoulder, and I followed. Our lips moved on each other. We hugged and pulled apart. Our eyes were three inches apart. We held a whole conversation up close like that.

"You wear Aramis," she whispered, her voice soft yet intimate. "It's one of my favorites."

I was tempted to ask how many other men wore the same scent.

"I've wanted to do this since I saw you this morning," she

continued, her fingers gently brushing through my curls. "I adore your curls and those captivating eyes. How old are you?"

I told her.

"You look nineteen, not twenty-one."

"How old are you?" I asked.

"Same as you."

Since Patty, all the important women in my life were older than me.

* * *

We never took more than the first sip of the beer. The anticipation crackled in the air like a live wire as we stumbled into my bedroom, our laughter mingling with the soft hum of the night. I mentioned wanting to shower, but Elena's eyes sparkled with a mischievous glint.

"I can't wait that long," she purred, her fingers already tugging at my T-shirt with an urgency that sent shivers down my spine.

In a whirlwind of passion, we tore each other's clothes off, the fabric falling to the floor in a chaotic heap. We collapsed onto the bedspread, our bodies entwined, the world outside forgotten. Elena straddled me, her lips a trail of fire as they moved from my forehead to my face, ears, chin, neck, and chest. Each kiss was a promise, a tantalizing hint of what was to come.

Her hands found mine, pinning them gently but firmly to the bed. She wanted control, and I was more than willing to surrender. This wasn't my first time; Ava and Emma had always insisted I relax and let them take the lead, but I had always made sure to return the favor before we were done. With Elena, though, there was an electric unpredictability that made my heart race.

I didn't know where this night would take us. Was this a

fleeting moment of passion, or was there something deeper at play? As her lips continued their descent, I realized that, for once, I didn't need to know. This wasn't about a job, a duty, or an obligation. This was about the raw, unfiltered connection between two people, and I was ready to lose myself in it.

The phone kept ringing. I let it ring. The caller was persistent.

We were heating up that bed. Elena had made it to command central, but that damn phone was still ringing. The fire between us was smoldering.

I was out of breath.

I picked up the phone and breathed. "Yes," I said.

"You must be busy," said a familiar voice.

"Yes," I said to Olivia.

* * *

An adjuster came by to inspect a customer's car that had been left for repairs. Normally, Ramirez handled the few adjusters who came over, but he wasn't in sight.

"Understand you're the owner," he said.

"And I understand you're the money-bags from Intrastate." We shook hands. "What's it take to get more business from your company?"

"You have a nice shop," he said, looking around.

"Lots of room not being used," I said. "We're big on painting, but I have two good body and fender men."

"Get some loan cars and send a letter to our chief adjuster. I'll give you a card before I go. He'll come down, look around, and I can't imagine he won't like the operation you have going here. No other shops around here are this clean and orderly."

"Thanks," I said.

*　*　*

The business was thriving, and I brought Elena on board, agreeing to pay her the minimum wage of fifty dollars per week.

"I wish I could pay more," I apologized.

"It's fine - I already told you not to worry," she reassured me before a spontaneous kiss passed between us.

"You're going to be a delightful distraction," I teased.

Her response was playful as she ran her tongue over her lips. "Not such a bad thing, is it?"

Amidst my bustling schedule, I often caught glimpses of Elena upstairs in the office. She would stand by the windows, at times engaged in phone conversations, other times lost in her own thoughts, occasionally indulging in a cigarette.

I began keeping the louvers closed, making it less obvious when Elena and I were spending time up there together. The two of us were like a fire pit that never stopped burning. Despite my efforts to avoid comparing the present with the past, my mind wouldn't cooperate. Selena and I had shared an intense, passionate relationship, always seeking out adventurous places for our escapades. In contrast, Elena and I didn't look for public spots to be intimate, but we certainly had our fair share of passionate moments, both day and night. It was the kind of fervor you'd expect from a pair of twenty-one-year-olds.

*　*　*

Elena had a visitor one day. I saw him coming in, and he caught my eye. He was dressed in a business suit but carried himself cooler than a businessman. His hair was on the long side, and he had some hair on his face. He came up to me and asked for Elena. He was a good-looking guy and at least twice my age. I noticed the speaking voice. There was something strong and controlled about it.

I called her on the intercom. Elena came down to the shop to meet him. He hugged and kissed her like a sailor who had just disembarked from a ship.

"This is Pepe," Elena said. "Pepe hosts three hours on a Mexican radio station."

That explained the voice. After she introduced us, and they walked together to the office upstairs and shut the door.

The next day, Pepe started plugging the one-day paint service at Brooklyn & Rowan. He never mentioned the price or the name of the shop, but Elena said he couldn't do that unless we were paying for commercial space.

It took a few days; then I began seeing the results. After a customer said she heard about us from Pepe on the radio, I told Ramirez to start asking how each customer heard about us. Did they drive by? Did a friend refer them? We should have been doing that before, but we were doing it now. In three days, we had eight cars. That's eight drivers who drove here just from Pepe's mention of the shop, not even saying the price of a paint job or the name of the shop.

"Thanks for the hookup with Pepe," I told Elena.

"I think you should buy a few commercials. I can talk to him for a special rate."

Pepe was smart. Before he tried to sell me, he had done something to prove how effective he was to his audience.

"Get me some prices," I said.

"I already have them. Let's discuss it tonight."

I kissed her.

"Deal," I said. I went downstairs.

Back to work

* * *

Pepe didn't own the radio station, but he had a lot to do with selling space for his three hours on the air, five days a week. He cut a deal with Elena to do twenty-one-minute spot commercials for two hundred[2] dollars. That was a lot of money back then, but it was nothing to what others paid for a spot. Elena assured me of this. I had no experience with advertising.

* * *

I took the insurance adjuster's advice and bought five fairly new police Plymouths that had a shitload of mileage. I had them painted in a bitching metallic silver that we could never do for thirty-five dollars, then I had my sign painter do a subtle sign on the front doors with the shop name, phone number, and in italics: *We offer loan cars.*

Ramirez loved the idea. He said that he once had two loaners. He complimented me on buying the cop cars at a steal. After I painted the Safeway manager's car for free, I parked the loaners at the Safeway parking lot in the spaces closest to the street across from my shop.

Elena and I were standing at the front entrance of the street, looking out. "The cars look sharp lined up like that," Elena said.

"I prefer that the cars are out with customers who have insurance repairs that we're doing."

"Give it a couple of days," she said, laughing. "You're remarkable," she said.

"Far from remarkable," I said, "but thanks."

"Let's go upstairs," she whispered.

It was almost six. I hardly needed to glance at my watch. I could tell the time because Ramirez was pacing. The deal was he couldn't get his Early Times until the shop was closed.

---

2. Adjusted for inflation, $200.00 in 1962 is equal to $1,713.16 in 2020.

"Let's go to the apartment, and we can devour each other," I said.

"I'll get my purse," she said.

The only problem I had with Elena was that no matter when we called it a night, I had to drive her home. Once, it was almost three in the morning.

"This house is my aunt's. If I start treating it like a hotel, she could throw me out."

"I don't mind driving you," I said.

Elena had been working for me for about two months when this Ramirez clone showed up. I mean, he was wearing jeans and a top, and he wasn't old, wasn't drunk, and wasn't smiling or doing that signature bow, but he had Ramirez's exact face and body minus half a century of hard living. The Ramirez clone got out of a car while I was writing an estimate and came at me like a dump truck. He sucker-punched me like I had done Danny, Clara's boyfriend.

The estimate clipboard and pen went flying in one direction, and I went another. I flew backward off my feet, landing on my butt and sliding across the floor like it had been greased with pork fat. I heard the Hispanic housewife I was attending screaming loud enough to break the sound barrier. I didn't waste any time getting back on my feet and tried to reassure the customer, but Ramirez-light was going off.

"You fucked my dad out of his business, and now you are fucking with Elena. She's mine, fool."

I dodged his kick, which missed me entirely, dodged again, or my nose would have been broken. His fist struck my cheek instead.

He yelled. He growled in frustration. His mistake was

running off. He tried storming out like he had stormed in. I wasn't having any of it. There was so much rage in my head there wasn't room for anything else. I was shaking with anger. Blood was running down my face from somewhere.

I was running on instinct. I grabbed his shoulder, swung him around to face me, and hit him so hard my right hand hurt for weeks. It was his turn to crash, only it wasn't his ass that broke his fall. He crashed into the concrete with his head.

I opened the passenger door of his car and shoved him halfway in his car while kicking his ass. Ramirez and two of my men pulled me off of him. If they hadn't, I don't know where that would have ended.

Ramirez took one look at his son and shoved me, but not hard enough to knock me off my feet.

"You hurt him," he yelled.

"Keep this animal away from me," I yelled back. "He won't be as lucky next time."

"You have no right to do this," Ramirez yelled at me. He was trying to comfort his son, who was slumped in his car's forward passenger seat.

I pointed at my bloody face.

"I didn't start this," I yelled. "Look at me. If I was a snitch, I'd have him arrested for assault. I've never seen him before in my life! What the fuck!"

Elena came sauntering from the office while smoking a cigarette. Halfway down the stairs, she stopped dead and looked at me. The cigarette went flying. Our eyes met, and I saw her eyes flick at Ramirez's clone's car.

"Loser!" she yelled, "You fucking loser, David!" she said, tearing down the stairs to mop the blood off my face with one of those trifold brown paper towels we used to clean the windows.

It was a crazy morning. Jesse and Chris came out of the meat market to check on me while I was in the men's room washing up. Elena was in the bathroom with me. The cut wasn't much, but I will never forget the bruised cheek and eye. Ramirez's son was taken to the ER for stitches on his head.

Luis and Felipe took care of the waiting customers.

"Go out and talk to the lady I was taking care of," I told Elena. "And her paint job is on the house. Give her a loaner if she doesn't want to wait."

Elena smiled, pinched my nose very gently, and went out to take care of business.

Chapter 15
Ramirez Splits

The only loss for me was that Ramirez never came back. He didn't have any personal belongings to come back for, but just like that, he was gone. He had one more month to finish up our deal.

Elena said she wanted to work the floor with me. She had already helped Ramirez and me when we got swamped, but now it was official. My gain.

* * *

Looking back with the twenty-twenty vision of hindsight, I figure that Ramirez had to be infuriated at himself and me. I swanned in, got a lease from the landlady, and got the body shop nearly rent-free because of the rental from the meat market. It freed me up to do so many essential things. I remodeled the grease pit that had been right under his nose for so many years, and it cost me very little out of pocket. I never showed him the numbers, but he had to know. He was smart, and it was his business. He never betrayed his jealousy unless the grinning and bowing was the way he expressed it. The best thing he did was leave when he did. It put pressure on me to learn the business on my own. I still can't say anything bad about Ramirez, contrary to everything I heard about him and the warnings given to me about him.

* * *

I told my team, "I had seriously considered letting him stay on longer." I waited and kept expecting him to show up, but he never came back.

"You don't need him," Elena said. "You got me."

He had done a lot, but I stepped into his shoes with Elena working beside me. My team of workers was growing, but I only hired someone when it was clear someone was needed. I was very careful with my overhead. Eventually, I hired Gil to work with Elena and me.

* * *

I didn't write a letter to Paul Anderson, the chief adjuster at Intrastate. I had Elena call and invite him to the shop instead. When he came over, I could have let my trainee Gil take over, but it was Elena whom I wanted to show him around. He seemed to like what he saw in the shop. We were busy. Our shop was clean, we had a waiting room and loan cars, and we were friendly. He put Eastland Auto Center on a list of preferred shops Intrastate recommended to their insureds who had an accident.

It didn't happen overnight, but we started getting big jobs, the kind that are towed in.

The insurance business was another sucker punch. I had to front the money for all the parts and labor. After delivering the car to the customer, I had to wait to get a check in the mail.

* * *

Elena answered phones and worked the floor with Gil and me. Her challenge was learning how to do estimates alongside Gil. She wore jeans like I did, but she had a jeans ass, and I didn't. She wore a T-shirt like me, but hers was colorful. She wore a bra to keep her nipples under wraps, but she looked great.

Elena began referring to me as G. "Is that okay with you?"

"I have no issue with it. In fact, someone else used to call me G before, but I can't recall who it was."

The nickname stuck, and my workers started calling me G. Even those who were not fluent in English adopted an English-inflected 'G' when addressing me.

"Teaching Elena and Gil made me smarter in the business. They trailed me like baby chicks. When I called dealers and junk yards to locate parts and prices, Gil and Elena watched every move I made. Having Elena on the shop floor added gusto to all of us. Carlos, my attorney, always counseled me not to make my employees my friends and to keep them at a distance so there is always respect, but I was the opposite. Aside from my ongoing relationship with Elena, I knew about every worker I had. I knew only what each one told me, but when I heard something, I remembered it. I knew how many kids each one had. My masker had two husbands, and my sander had two wives. Their lives were a drama in mid-performance. We worked together as many hours as necessary. I put them all on payroll, but it was formulated. If my painter made fifty dollars for the week, half of that was a paycheck with deductions. Half was cash. That's what they insisted on.

***

When Ramirez wanted me to hustle the car dealers on Atlantic Boulevard, I did it. I passed cards around and a foldout brochure with pictures of the spray booth, oven, and shop. For a while, a dealer would call. Elena would have to tell them we were too busy to take the job and sweet-talk the caller not to write us off. We were that busy. But being busy didn't mean the shop was out of space. I had space for a mechanic to work on two cars at a time, two upholstery workers to set up shop with their material samples displayed on a wall, and even a wheel alignment set up. I had planned it all with Luis, who knew every bit of the industry.

Elena said, "G, wait. Take it slow. My mom told me once she could have opened eight mortuaries, and instead, she only opened two because she knew she could watch two operations but not eight."

"Your mom told you that?"

"She did. She wanted me to work in the mortuary when I was a little kid. She didn't want me to be afraid."

I swallowed and laughed.

"Elena, sometimes, I wonder if you always tell the truth."

"G, I never lie."

***

One time after work, we were at my apartment eating take-out. The aroma of spicy Szechuan chicken and sweet and sour pork filled the room, mingling with the faint scent of jasmine from the candle burning on the coffee table. The greasy feel of the take-out containers contrasted with the smooth, cool surface of the wooden table beneath them.

"Did you screw Pepe, the radio guy?" I asked, my voice barely audible over the crunch of crispy spring rolls.

"I didn't screw him. I fucked him," Elena replied her words as sharp and direct as the tangy bite of the hot mustard sauce. That's how Elena was. She didn't mince words.

"Did fucking him have anything to do with the special pricing he gave me to advertise on his station?" I asked, the taste of soy sauce lingering on my tongue.

She laughed, a sound as light and effervescent as the bubbles in the soda we were drinking. "Had nothing to do with that."

"If you had said yes, I'd feel bad," I said, feeling the cool condensation from the soda can against my palm.

"Are you okay with it?" she asked, her eyes searching mine.

I shrugged, the fabric of my shirt rustling softly. "It's done, past tense."

"Just like that?" she pressed, her voice carrying a hint of the sweet and sour sauce we had just eaten.

I shrugged again, feeling the weight of the conversation lift slightly. "What can I say." I smiled, the taste of our meal still lingering in the air.

* * *

Elena was a people person. She got along with lady customers like I couldn't believe. She complimented how they were dressed, how great their complexion was, or the shade of lipstick they were wearing. Elena could sell.

I gave her a raise. "I'm with you all the time. I got no bills and no time or need to buy clothes, but thanks for the extra."

We were getting close. She asked about my father in Arizona and my stepdad, Leonard. I asked her why her aunt was running the mortuaries.

"My mom owned the mortuaries, but my aunt always did the

work. I have a brother, seven years older than me," Elena said. "He took over the mortuaries, at least technically. My aunt just kept doing what she was doing when my mother was alive. Someday my brother will take it over, but he's lazy. Legally, they belong to my brother. As far as I know, I got nothing coming. I get zero unless I count a very nice bedroom at my aunt's house, and if I want anything to eat, she makes sure I have it."

"Wow," I said. "I didn't mean to dig that deep."

"I like the word dig," she said, kissing me. Her lips were soft and tasted faintly of the cherry lip balm she always used. "Are you ready?" She was feeling me, her touch warm and electric.

"I stay ready."

I loved the way she kissed me. Her kisses were complex, her own, and hard to explain. They were a mix of gentle and passionate, leaving a lingering taste of sweetness and a hint of the coffee she had earlier. Her touch was both comforting and exciting, making my skin tingle with every caress.

* * *

I got it from the team grapevine that Ramirez had opened a small shop on Olympic Boulevard. His son David was working with him.

"I'm happy for him," I said.

The truth is that I missed Ramirez. I missed the grin, the bows, his laugh. I could understand his feelings when he saw his son bleeding, but what about me? I didn't start the fight. I don't know why I was so mournful about it. I mean, at some point, Ramirez would have split. It was only a month early. It was too bad he left the way he did. I felt guilty.

I bought a television and installed an antenna on the shop's roof, and wham, we had a television. Elena and I sometimes spent time up in the office after the shop was closed. We had a couch and a chair. Compared to my apartment, the office was the most uncomfortable place to be.

Elena bought a bottle of Canadian Club one night and poured us a drink using seven-up. It was tasty and smooth, not at all like the gut-wrenching Presidente that I drank straight in Juarez. Soon I kept Canadian Club at home, but I don't remember sitting around alone and drinking. I do remember that when I realized that the seven-up was inflating me, I switched to water. It was my staple drink for decades to come.

* * *

In those intimate moments with Elena, her skin exuded a smooth, elastic radiance, releasing a captivating fragrance that mingled with our lovemaking. Although I can't recall the brand of her perfume, its unique scent is etched in my memory—a blend of jasmine and sandalwood, with a hint of citrus—that I would recognize instantly even today. Elena was a mesmerizing blend of the irresistible qualities of Patty, Alicia, Clara, Ava, and Emma, with perhaps a touch of Selena and Luna, embodying the sultry and provocative allure of each of these remarkable women.

Like Selena, but not as intense, Elena had a streak of madness. I had some of that too. If we hung around at the office instead of driving to my apartment, we'd do strange things to each other. Once in a while, my painter would leave a car in the spray booth, ready to paint in the morning. Ready to paint means the windows are all covered with brown wrapping paper, and the chrome is taped with masking tape. The bumpers are covered completely with paper wrap and tape, and the body of the car has been cleaned with cheesecloth, so there is absolutely no dust on it when the paint is applied.

Elena and I would go into the spray booth and make our own

adventure in whatever we found there. If the car was a four-door, we'd open the back door, climb in, and go at each other ferociously. The confined space amplified our passion, the scent of fresh paint mingling with our own. Same for a two-door if it didn't have a console. Bucket seats were a challenge, especially in a tiny foreign car. The aroma in the car was more sensual than after sex in a bedroom—a mix of leather, paint, and our own musk. Sometimes it felt like we were making love in a clown car. Once in a while, there was a van. Vans were special. In those days, they were just starting to make vans into moving bedrooms with shag carpeting on the ceiling and walls, and op art posters that made you say things like "groovy" and "far out." The plush carpet felt soft against our skin, and the psychedelic patterns on the walls seemed to pulse with our movements. When we were spent, we'd laugh and laugh. We'd kiss and hug like we were madly in love, the echoes of our laughter bouncing off the van's walls.

* * *

We were savoring take-out tacos from the meat market next door. Each day, as we shared these meals, I found myself uncovering more about Elena—though only the pieces she chose to reveal. Our lunch was on paper plates perched on chairs, using my desk as our makeshift table.

"Have you tried their new salsa?" Elena asked, pushing a container in my direction. "Jesse said they made it fresh today from their grandmother's recipe."

I spooned some into the taco. "Not bad. I taste the lime."

I don't know what made a connection in Elena's head. Maybe the lime.

Out of the blue, she said, "Did I tell you I used to work at the Brooklyn Street Mortuary after my mom died?"

"I don't remember exactly what you said, maybe something about your mom didn't want you to be afraid of being at the mortuary or something."

"That too, but that's when I was a kid. When I was in high school, I worked at the office, stopped working for a while, and went back to work when I graduated. Want to know why I finally quit?"

I put down my taco and looked at her. "I want to know, yeah?"

"I couldn't stand the crying. I was in an office, away from the interviewer's offices, but I could still hear the loved ones' cries, screams, and sobs. I was a nervous wreck. I told my aunt I couldn't handle it. She wanted me to suck it up and grow a spine. She told me I should grow a tougher skin because I had to work to live. I had to learn to ignore it to put money in my purse."

"Gross. I'm sorry you went through that."

"G, it's not gross. It's sad."

I put my third taco back on the plate. "I'm sorry. I used the wrong word. I think of the mortuary part of it as gross."

Elena didn't smile.

She paused mid-bite, her gaze drifting into the distance as if lost in thought. Moments later, she blinked out of her reverie, and a familiar smile returned, brighter and more radiant than before. It was as if a light had flickered back to life within her, drawing me in all over again.

It was Sunday evening, and I had gone to Shakey's to pick up a pizza. Elena was on my bed, watching television with a heating pad. As I unlocked the door, I heard the theme music of Walt Disney's Wonderful World of Color. It was a bad time of the month for her. I carried the pizza box, paper plate, and a hundred paper napkins into the bedroom.

I'd thought Disney would cheer her up, but she was sobbing uncontrollably.

"What's wrong?" I said, sitting down beside her.

She looked at me sadly, tears streaming. "Bambi's Mama died."

"Aww," I said, making a move to get up and turn it off.

"Don't you dare," she said, catching my arm. "Let's watch the movie."

After it was over, Elena apologized for getting emotional.

"Hey," I said," It was a sad scene. You'd have to have a heart of stone not to cry. Bambi is a cool kind of hero. For a deer."

She looked a little spaced out. "I never told you how my mom died?"

"No, you haven't."

"Everyone who knew her has a different rumor of what happened to my mom. Some of them are probably correct."

I got up and turned off the TV. She was looking at it, but all I turned off was a dish soap commercial. I sat back beside her, not turning to face her. She kept looking ahead, but I knew she was not watching the TV, which was off.

"My mom She overdosed."

Silence. I didn't know what to say. "Elena, it's not enough for me to simply say how sorry I am to hear that."

She turned to face me. Her eyes were moist.

"I'm sorry, too," she whispered. I took her in my arms, and her face rested on my shoulder.

"I'm sorry about the tears. I get all sad when I'm on my period."

We embraced, lost in each other. "Baby, I'm here for you."

* * *

I never married Elena, but our bond was deep, akin to that of a committed couple. Despite any lingering feelings for her exes, she kept them to herself, a silent testament to her loyalty. While I cherished Elena's presence, I also longed for Olivia and my two working girlfriends who lived nearby. Eventually, I introduced the latter to Elena, carefully omitting their profession.

When she met Ava and Emma, Elena's eyes sparkled with curiosity. "I'm sure you've had some wild times with them. They're attractive! What's their going rate?" she remarked, her voice tinged with playful mischief.

Perplexed, I furrowed my brow and asked, "What do you mean by 'going rate?'"

Amused, Elena let out a melodic laugh that echoed in the room. "You know what I mean," she clarified, her eyes dancing with amusement.

Olivia, on the other hand, never came around without an invite. I never got the opportunity to introduce her to Elena, a small regret that lingered in the back of my mind.

Elena and I worked hard when we weren't playing hard. Behind every scene is a six in the morning opening that ended when we closed between six and seven. That's a long day. Elena laughed at how easy it was to sell paint jobs. She was doing fine estimating the nicks and bangs that customers wanted taken care of now that they were painting their car. Elena was a jack of all trades. She hadn't told me that when I interviewed her for the job. I hired her mainly for her fine looks, but that lady was a prize.

Gil was older than Elena and me. He was a fast learner who wanted to fit in. His Spanish was not very good, but we were there to save him if the customer spoke no English. His zeal reminded me of my mom and her struggle to learn how to speak, write, and read English.

* * *

Sitting at my desk and opening the mail, Elena said, "We billed the insurance 42 days ago, and just now, Bingo - we got the check!"

"It sure feels good when it comes in," I said.

I remember the first insurance check I finally received in the mail. It was for $945, which was a lot of money then.

Elena wasn't excited like I was.

She pulled out a calendar and looked at the check, frowning, but we had customers. We went down and set up a couple of paint jobs and some bodywork. Later, when we had time between customers, Elena went upstairs and was back with a calculator tape.

"You have nine invoices out to Intrastate and Hartford. A total of $6,450 dollars.[1] G, this is big money, not thirty-five dollars for a paint job."

"I know," I said. "If we didn't have the flow from the paint-work, I wouldn't be able to pay for the parts and material to put out the insurance jobs. It's deadly."

That night, we were at my apartment. We'd drank maybe three CC Waters. We were not drunk, but we were loose.

Elena said, "You would make more money in the mortuary business. You don't have to bill in that business. Everything is paid upfront."

I laughed.

I hugged her.

---

1. Adjusted for inflation, $6,450.00 in 1962 is equal to $55,249.41 in 2020.

I kissed her, and she hugged and kissed me back and joined me in laughter.

"I wanted so much to do insurance work, and now that I'm getting it, I don't have the balls to turn it away. I have deep reservations about continuing."

Elena smiled, reached between my legs, and grabbed, not hard, but enough to get my attention. "You have balls. Shut the insurance work down unless they can pay you when the car is finished."

"You met the player from Intrastate, Hartford, and Farmers. They warned us we had to bill and wait."

"Farmers said they are working on issuing a check payable to the insured and the body shop, and when the work is finished, the customer gives us the check, and that's it."

"I'd love that," I said.

"I'll call the adjuster, Mike, and ask him if that is happening or if it is bullshit."

I couldn't get drunk because being drunk was not fun for me and also because Elena would want to go home to sleep, but I guess that didn't stop me.

"I feel so good," she said. "Let's have another drink."

"I like the way you make them," I said.

"Coming up," she said.

At three or so in the morning, Elena got out of bed, dressed, and called a taxi. Los Angeles was a taxi city back then. Yellow Cabs were everywhere. A cab took Elena home, and I slept like a baby.

I had no hangover like the one I'd had in Juarez, but then, I didn't drink that much, and I was older now than in Juarez. Does that make a difference?

Fifteen minutes before eight, my crew was outside the Brooklyn Avenue entrance. I drove up and parked my car in a reserved spot. Jesse and Chris also had a reserved spot. I unlocked the gates. Felipe and Emily pushed the heavy gates open.

"Emily, let Manual do that. You're too fine a lady to be pushing heavy gates."

"You so out of sight, boss," she said. She was wearing her standard jeans and tee, but she put on her uniform to paint or mask. Her hair was up in a ponytail.

Elena walked in, rolled her eyes at me, and put her hand on her hip.

"Stop flirting, G."

She waved at Emily.

I kissed Elena with gusto. It didn't matter who was watching.

"You look great," I said. What she could do in a pair of jeans could just break your heart.

"You do too," she said with a kiss.

She moved cars in and out of the shop all the time. "I know you can drive," I said.

"I drive. I have a driver's license and everything. You gonna buy me a car or something?"

"You should have taken my car last night. I feel bad you took a cab."

"How would you have gotten here this morning?"

"You could have picked me up."

"I'll take you up on that next time," she said. "I love your wheels."

"That makes two of us," I said, walking over to the bench to get my clipboard. Three customers made an appearance in the parking lot next to the entrance.

"I been known to drive a hearse," Elena said, laughing, clipboard in hand. "You gonna get me a hearse?"

Gil walked in exactly at eight, opening time.

Chapter 16
Lunch Together a Must

We always made time for lunch together. Paint jobs normally came in the morning, and we promised one-day delivery of up to ten cars. We didn't always hit the magic ten, but most times, we did. I'd say that only half of the customers expected one day service. If there was bodywork to do, we got an extra day for that. Customers didn't mind.

"Did you really drive a hearse?"

"Fuckin' A. Four times."

"Why?"

"We were shorthanded. I put a suit on the janitor, and he rode shotgun with me and did any heavy work that needed to be done. I know the drill. Nothing to it."

"I keep learning about you, something new every day. I look forward to the next revelation."

* * *

Elena and I ate way too much Mexican food from the market next door. The taco guy would make whatever I wanted. Sometimes I ordered a steak that Jesse would cut up special for me. But we had burritos and tacos more often. We weren't fat because we worked hard and fucked hard and I jogged every morning.

We were eating on the sofa, the food between us.

"You don't talk about yourself, ever," Elena said, taking a small bite of a jalapeño.

"At my age, how much past do I have?"

She snorted. "Way more than you let on. Here's what I know. You are married, have one baby daughter, and you have been married twice before the present wife."

She put the jalapeño up to my lips. I swallowed it.

"Hot like your pussy," I said, sucking in some air that didn't cool the burn. It was a good burn, though.

"You nasty, G."

"You don't like nasty?"

"I love nasty."

My attorney, Carlos, referred me to an accountant who was a certified public accountant. I didn't know the difference in the titles, but I would learn. His name was Donald. Like Carlos, I could walk to his office on Brooklyn Avenue. He was the same guy Elena had told me about.

Elena had been right. There was no need for me to keep track of the state tax collected on invoices. Donald did it. First, he came over and set up a system for us to follow with sales invoices, parts purchased on credit, and parts purchased with cash. Then he came over once a week. He got into the business account I had at Holmberg's bank and reconciled the account. It was all Greek to me initially, but I paid attention. Just like I learned some heavy-duty tasks while working with Matt, just like I learned around Ramirez, I got the hang of the accounting. I had no choice. I didn't have Ramirez anymore. I learned by trial and error. Once Donald got it all set up, he said he'd come in once a month. He assured me he was a phone call away for anything I needed.

Donald was a little paunchy and soft from his sedentary job. With his Benjamin Franklin eyeglasses and a receding hairline, he looked like a mild-mannered guy, but he had a brain like a steel trap behind those frames. He was nobody's fool. He was very paternal toward me. I should have listened better to all his advice. I was game to learn the mechanics but listening to anyone's advice was a different story.

"You have twenty thousand and change in accounts receivable from insurance companies. You have fifteen thousand in the bank, and I have eight thousand in bills to pay for parts and other purchases." He shook his head.

"Don, write the checks. The money is in the bank. I already paid the rent and the lights, and the payroll account has enough for three payrolls, even without any more deposits."

"I worry about you," he said. "It was a garbage pit for years. You made something out of this corner. You are smart. I don't want you to make mistakes I can see coming down the road."

"Don, I love you. I'm being careful."

"Okay," he said. "Remember, cash and carry are better than credit."

When Don was here on his regular visit, he always sat at my desk upstairs, the same desk Elena used when she was in the office doing work.

"I got to get downstairs," I said. "Want me to send you up tacos at lunchtime?"

Donald jumped at the offer. "No need to wait for lunch. I'm starving."

"You got it," I said.

* * *

Cars were coming in. Cars had to be painted. With all the insurance work, more cars were being towed in that needed serious bodywork and new parts. I had no choice. I hired another bodyman, Mando, recommended by Luis and Felipe, who knew and recommended him. Then, I had to hire a bodyman assistant. One man can't dismantle a badly wrecked car. Even with two, it's time-consuming. The helper came in and was paid just over one dollar an hour. I looked at forty a week as two paint jobs at thirty-five dollars. There is a cost factor to put out a thirty-five-dollar paint job. It was crazy the way I thought then, but looking back, I was on the right track. The problem would be that I wasn't paying attention to reality.

* * *

So, I was doing the usual, taking in customers, setting someone up for her car to be prepped and painted, and I saw this gorgeous chic standing among customers' cars. She was looking my way and waving and smiling. I handed my clipboard to Gil and double-timed towards her. She actually opened her arms, and I went in them. I didn't see the expression on Elena's face, but she was close by.

I introduced her to Elena.

"This is Clara, my second wife's roommate," I said. "She's married to a guy named Danny."

Elena hugged Clara, the fox.

"I heard you opened up a shop or something. I was heading

to a job interview on Atlantic at a car dealer, and soon as I saw this, I made a U-turn. I knew it was you."

She was almost dressed for an interview. She was wearing an expensive suit like you'd expect to wear at an office, only it was hot pink, and her top was unbuttoned about four inches below what a strait-laced female hiring manager would allow. It was super short, but everybody wore minis these days. Maybe she'd unbuttoned for my benefit. She was wearing clunky pink heels that looked like they weighed thirty pounds each. Clunky was the style too, but not so great on walking around on the pavement and the cement shop floor.

"It was nice meeting you," Elena said, looking at a businessman type who had just driven in behind a tow truck. "I have work to do, but I'd love to have a coffee and gossip about George's mysterious history." She laughed, did a little finger wave, and left.

"I have two questions," I said to Clara. "How did you know it was me? I never had a body shop before."

Clara flashed me that hot smile I remembered.

"Alicia told me you opened a body shop. She heard it on the radio but couldn't remember where on Brooklyn Avenue it was."

"I'm happy you drove in," I said.

"Next question?" she asked.

"Why did you quit Bullocks?"

"I quit before they got around to firing me for missing too much work. I have been on disability, but that runs out next week. I'm going to hustle for a job, like a receptionist or something. Danny brings home good money, so we're okay."

I walked her to the car and kissed her before she got in.

"I miss you," I said.

"You never call. I have the same number."

I smiled at my good friend.

She craned her neck to see out the window where Elena was talking to the tow driver and the businessman, looking fantastic, and keeping smiles on the faces of both men she was talking to.

"Is that your new girlfriend?" she asked, her eyebrow arching with curiosity.

"We're just good friends," I replied.

"Still into three on the bed?" she teased, a mischievous glint in her eye.

"You're irresistible," I said with a playful grin, my eyes locking onto hers.

Clara slowly licked her lips, her gaze never wavering.

Clara was looking at me like I was one of those spicy tacos from the guy who drove the lunch truck by all the department stores. "I know how that goes."

And then she was gone.

Chapter 17
No Secrets

Elena and I didn't drink a lot, but we drank regularly. I seldom drank beer anymore. Elena didn't like beer. We were on the sofa in front of the TV. No telling now what we were watching. We often had the television on with the volume turned way down, equivalent now to mute.

"Tell me about your friend Clara."

"She's a doll, isn't she?"

"A doll," Elena said, raising her glass.

"Not as pretty as you, but a doll just the same. We used to have a lot of fun."

"She lived with your second wife?"

"My second wife was Alicia. When I met her, she was living with Clara in the City of Commerce. We had good times together."

Elena gave me a little shove. "I can only imagine. Did you have something going with both, then you married one?"

I gave her a little shove back.

She laughed with her whole body. She had a lot of different laughs, and I liked all of them.

"I had a crush on Alicia, the one I married. It lasted twenty-eight days."

"So, you said."

"I spent a year around the two of them. If we hadn't gotten married, we'd probably still be tight." Then I thought about it. "Maybe not. I met Alicia after she broke up with a guy. She ended up back with him when we got divorced. It's complicated. My whole life is complicated."

"We're twenty-one. How complicated could it be?"

"Well, he drove her to Mexico for the divorce."

She shrugged.

"That's not complicated."

I did what she did to me all the time. I stroked her hair with my hand.

"While you were busy working on a high school diploma, I was in prison," I said, my voice barely above a whisper, the weight of my admission hanging in the air.

Elena looked at me, her eyes widening like saucers and her mouth forming a perfect 'o.' The room seemed to hold its breath.

"You? Not a chance," she said, her voice tinged with disbelief.

"I'll tell you another night," I replied, my gaze dropping to the floor.

"George, I'm sorry. Is it true?" she asked, her voice softer now, almost a whisper. She tipped her glass, but it was empty. The ice clinked softly as she set it down on the end table. I took a sip of my drink, the cool liquid burning slightly as it went down, and she took it out of my hand. She took a sip, her lips lingering on the rim of the glass.

"It's true." I reached out and touched her face, my fingers tracing the curve of her cheek. "I don't know why I told you."

"It's you and me, G. I have explored your entire body with my mouth. You have explored me. How can there be any secrets?

I told you about my mom. You weren't there. You didn't know, and I told you," she said, her voice trembling slightly.

"I like the way you include body exploration to secrets." I chuckled, trying to lighten the mood.

"Stop making fun," she teased, a small smile playing on her lips.

I never hide my past," I said. "Never. I just hadn't got around to telling you about it. It's not a secret. I'm over it. It's no big deal to me anymore."

"I want you right now," Elena said, her voice husky with desire.

"Not as much as I want you," I replied, my voice equally thick with longing. We reached for the light, and our hands touched as we both turned it off. The room was plunged into darkness, the only sound the soft hum of the TV. I flicked it off, and we headed for bed, the anticipation crackling between us like static electricity.

* * *

I checked in with Sophia once or twice a week on the phone. I wasn't as good about going over as before.

It was always the same call:

"How are you? How is Judy?"

The same reply:

"Everything is okay."

This time, Sophia said something new.

"When you are thinking about coming over, please do, but call first."

Sophia had never said that before. I figured she was pissed off because I had not been over to see Judy. She had the right to be pissed off.

"Any reason why I need to make an appointment?"

Straight forward, Sophia said, "There is a reason. Sometimes I have a friend visiting."

I digested that in silence. I spoke up before the pause went on too long.

"Of course, I will call before," I said.

Sophia said, "I have been thinking about moving to my grandparents' house. That will take this financial load off you."

"You do what you think is right but don't do it because you want to relieve me of the expenses I'm paying. You have it coming."

Silence then. "Thanks, George. How many more months are left on the house lease?"

"Not sure. I'll check and let you know."

"Don't renew it unless we talk first."

"You'll know because you need to sign the renewal, too," I reminded her.

"I won't sign a renewal," she said with finality.

I told Elena all the pieces of my life she had not known about. It took about a week to bring her up to speed. She had known how many times I'd been married but nothing about my wives, prison, or any of the details. Nothing about my first wife Selena, me running off from the Navy, Mexico, the FBI, the brig, and DVI. I told her in segments, like chapters in a book. I told her about the locker thing but not the drugstore thing.

I know we were feeling close that week. We were busy as busy gets, with a line going out the door, people waiting inside to pick up their cars, and everyone working at the top of their game. The air was thick with the scent of motor oil and fresh paint, mingling with the distant hum of engines and the clatter of tools. Elena caught me looking at her and left her customer.

"Can I see you a moment?" she asked, her expression telegraphing that it was something urgent.

"Excuse me," I told my customer, Mrs. Quinn. "Take a look at the samples and think about the color you want."

I put my hand up, and Gil came over to show her his swatches while she was looking at the paint colors. Elena took my hand, and we stopped at the foot of the office stairs. The metal steps were cool under my fingers as I leaned against the railing.

She turned to face me, her eyes penetrating. Something was wrong. She put her arms around my neck. I could feel her warm breath on the nape of my neck, and her fragrance embraced me. It gave me a shiver down my spine. Her perfume was a mix of jasmine and something sweet, like vanilla.

"I feel so close to you," she said, her voice barely above a whisper.

"Thanks for that," I said. I want to love you, Elena, but love for me always ends in a failed marriage."

"You love me," she said. "You just don't know it yet."

We kissed, and when I got back to my customer, I had to wipe my eyes on my sleeve. The taste of her lingered on my lips, a blend of mint and something uniquely Elena.

When the morning rush was over, long before we broke for lunch, we went up to the office, not to have sex. We were high on each other. I don't know how long we stood up there, hugging each other, breathing on each other, in silence. The room was filled with the soft hum of the air conditioner and the distant sounds of the shop below.

"Love would ruin this great relationship we have," I said. "I feel complete, happy being with you like we are."

Then one day, she said, "You don't have to love me. But is it okay if I love you?"

"Are you preparing me for a joke?" She did like to joke around.

"No joke," she laughed. "I love you, G. We spend all our time together. I get all goosebumps when we touch. I know I love you."

I felt dizzy and closed my eyes. My life was too complicated to add a new complexity. The room seemed to spin, the walls closing in for a moment.

"You seem worried," she chuckled. "Today is what matters. Tomorrow is unpredictable." Then she continued, "Stop assuming that loving me means we'll eventually get married."

"Three marriages have gone down the tubes for me," I reminded her. "I've always been so insecure that I felt marriage was the only way to hang on to wives one, two, and three."

"G, stop with the marriage thing already," she said with a big smile. "I'm not looking to get married."

"It would be my honor to marry you someday. You're the complete package. But I'd find a way to mess it up."

"G, stop already."

"When I was in Juarez, a fugitive wanted by the FBI for being AWOL from the Navy, I was a saint. I never messed around with another woman, not even once. I told you the story. One day, I found out that Selena, my wife, was seeing her ex-boyfriend and meeting him at a local hotel. A few hours after I found out about the double cross, I fucked Selena's sister in the backseat of her father's car, my father-in-law no less."

"G, I don't care if you mess around. That doesn't mean you can't love me. I mess around too."

I chuckled. "I have a headache; my brain is trying to keep up."

Elena laughed, a sound like wind chimes on a breezy day.

"I like strange just as much as you," she said.

"So we're both unfit," I said, though I knew I didn't look serious.

I kissed her, feeling the warmth of her lips and the electric connection between us.

* * *

Elena and I were at my apartment. She was in the shower. The phone rang.

I turned off the TV. I could still hear Elena singing in the shower, but not loud enough to make the phone hard to hear. I accepted the long-distance call from Tracy California.

"Hey! George. It's me, Mike."

"I just got out. I understand you're in business. Got a job for an old friend?"

I felt obligated, even though it was I who had saved his life once and not the other way around.

"Come over, and we'll talk."

I gave him the shop address. DVI gives you a little cash and a Greyhound ticket home. He was waiting for the bus, just as I had done once.

He called me the next night and said he'd met a girl on the bus and had gone home with her. She lived in West Los Angeles.

"She has a body to die for," he said. I heard her giggling in the background.

"I'll see you in a couple of days," he said. "Is that okay?"

"Tell him a week. You're going to be busy with my body shop before you move on to his," the girl said in the background, making me laugh.

"Don't worry, I'll be here. She sounds willing and happy to put you to work polishing her dents, peaks, valleys, and crevices."

"Gotta love those peaks and valleys," Mike said. "It's been a long time. Thanks, man. Later."

I remembered when I met Alicia right after I got out, got home, and got a car. I remember how badly I needed it when I got laid after more than two years. I knew how Mike felt, though he might have had it worse. He'd done more time than me.

* * *

The next day, we were having lunch, our eyes locked. We were on the sofa in my office, and most times, food plates between us. She was in her bell bottoms, legs crossed. My feet were flat on the floor.

"Are you going to hire him or help him out with some money?" Elena asked.

"He's smart and personable. He's got biceps out here," I illustrated with my hands. "He may want to take you away from me," I said with a grin.

"Oh, are you saying I'm yours?"

"I wish you were mine," I heard myself say.

Later we were on the shop floor watching Gil talk to a walk-in.

"Gil is doing great. If we can train Mike too, we could take off when we want and leave them to do the intake and handle the finished cars," I said.

"He may not even want to do that," Elena said. "You may not want him doing that."

"He doesn't look like a murderer or a criminal. He's our age. He's shacking up with a girl he met on the bus coming home from prison."

"It's your place, G, but I think it's too soon for you to turn the driving to others when you and I are not here."

"It's down the road. Learning this stuff is tricky."

"My mother worked the mortuary for years before she let my aunt run the operation, and then they opened a second place. My mother and aunt worked hours between both. When I'd complain she was never home, she'd apologize and tell me the family business could not operate without her. Told me to come see her at the business."

"Hey," I said. "The mortuary. That was then. This is now. You and me, we're here, kicking ass."

"And digging it," she said, licking her lips. She did that a lot.

"Best thing that happened to me was the day you came up to me looking for a job."

"You hired me to get in my panties, then you found out I had brains."

"I tell myself the same thing about you all the time."

"I know," she said.

"You do?"

* * *

One weekend we were out in the pool, and it started to rain. We came in at a run. Elena tore through the house ahead of me. I didn't know where she'd gone. Then I heard a creak and realized she was hiding in the closet of the second bedroom. I pretended to keep calling her, but I stood beside the closet and held the door shut. It was all a game, hide and seek, kind of, but she flipped out when she tried the door, and I was holding it shut.

"Open it now, George, and I'm not kidding."

Her voice was panicky. I opened it immediately, or at least as soon as I realized how freaked out she was.

Still in her wet bikini, she walked out of the closet and into the second bathroom she used the most and snagged a towel to dry off with. Her voice shook a little as she asked me, "Did I tell you the time my brother put me in a coffin?"

"No way."

"He's such a bastard. I was twelve or so. He was a bully, always joking around. He worked at the business after school. He said, 'Let's play hide and seek.' I was all for that until he went into the coffin room. It was the showroom, a big room with sample coffins, all types, and prices. I barely walked in; the lights were all on, and I didn't see him until he sprang out from behind the door I had opened. I screamed."

Elena's fair skin got flushed as she was telling me the story.

"Go on already," I said.

"The scumbag picked me up, laughing like it was all fun and games, and he put me down inside a coffin. The top was open, but it was too high for me to jump out. I started crying. Then he hit the switch, and the lights went out."

"Is this for real?"

"Oh, shut up, G. Fuckin' A it's for real. I'm not done yet."

"Go for it," I said, not sure what was coming or how to respond to it.

"I was screaming, lights were still out, and suddenly he yanked me out of the coffin and was acting like he was a ghost or saw a ghost or something. Finally, he set me down and turned the lights back on. I looked down at where I was standing and saw I had peed."

I looked over her shoulder through the bathroom door at the open closet.

"You didn't just pee in my closet, did you?"

She gave an unexpected bark of laughter and punched me in the shoulder.

"You know just the right thing to say." She gave a little hiccup and laughed again.

"Poor baby," I said. "That brother of yours was clearly a jerk. If it upsets you, why tell the story?"

"I'm not upset now," she said. "Ask me if I was upset then."

"You peed," I said. "That tells me everything I need to know."

"I went running to tell my aunt what happened. I was dying of embarrassment that I had peed, my panties and my skirt all wet. I was furious. My aunt said, 'Let's get you home to shower and dress.' She told me not to be afraid of coffins; they were just boxes. I never found out if my brother got scolded or what. I told my mom about it later. She was too busy to be sympathetic. She did want to make sure I told the housekeeper that the clothes had urine on them so she'd know how to wash them."

"Wow," I said. "Baby, you are full of stories."

"Yeah. So are you."

* * *

Don came by to do the books. He was looking more tanned than usual. I guess he'd taken a vacation or something or had maybe spent a weekend at the beach. I didn't ask.

"George, your receivables are going up, and so are your payables," he said. "Have you asked your bank about financing the accounts receivable?"

"You mean the insurance money that I'm owed?"

"Yes."

"Holmberg says his bank doesn't do that kind of financing. He can give me a loan for $3,000, but that's a personal loan."

"That would help."

"I owe him for equipment. My payments are small, and the door is wide open for me to go buy more equipment, and he'll finance it. I'm thinking I'll open a second shop one day."

"You didn't take him up on the three thousand?"

"I said no. I don't want personal loans like that. The three will go out in a whiff, and I'll be stuck owing the bank another three thousand with nothing to show for it. From the money I owe the bank now, I have a spray booth, I have an oven. I didn't have to pay my parents the three thousand so fast, but it bothered me to no end to owe them."

Don raised his hand to interrupt me.

"I understand. Let me finish up the numbers, and I'll come get you when I'm ready to lay it out for you."

"Don won't let up about the insurance work," I told Elena.

"G. I can call and put a pause on taking any new business from the insurance guys. I'll tell them the truth. We can't carry the paper right now."

"If we didn't paint so many cars, I couldn't begin to do the insurance work," I said. "If only we could paint more than ten cars a day. What if I get another shop?"

I went downstairs. Elena followed me to the Brooklyn entrance, where I was waiting for a customer to pick up his car.

Elena ruffled my hair.

"You don't want another shop," she said. "Wait until you got it all together."

"You mean like having more money?"

"Exactly. I was a kid when my mom opened the second mortuary, but she only opened it because she could afford it. It's just my opinion. I sure never discussed things like that with her at ten years old."

"Opening a body shop is not nearly as costly as opening a mortuary, I'm sure of it."

We had moved into the parking lot, where there was a nice breeze. I watched it blow through her silky hair. I look back now and wonder what others thought of us in moments like that. Everyone around us was busy, but the boss and his girlfriend were just standing there. Elena was ruffling my hair, and we were laughing together as if we were alone. We were so young.

Elena had a faraway look on her face as she turned and looked at the big sign.

"Well then, go find another spot."

"You don't mean that do you?"

"Fuck no. I don't mean it at all. Only a fool would do it now. You're not a fool."

"Say fuck again," I said.

"Donald is in the office. We can't just go fuck up there with him sitting at the desk."

"Can't we?" I laughed.

"I think he'd notice," she said.

"We should have a decent hotel around here for fucking emergencies," I said.

She let out a peal of laughter and was still laughing when a customer was dropped off to get her car. Elena took the customer to pick up the car. I got the next walk-in, leaving Gil ready to serve the next customer that came.

Chapter 18
Cash Flow Blues

Don wrote all checks due to suppliers, the sales tax I had collected that was due to the State Board of Equalization, and payroll taxes. I would write paychecks like I always did, following a guide that Don left me for tax deductions and all that.

"Your money at the bank will be skinny when these checks clear," he said. "I was surprised you have enough to handle it all."

"Thank goodness I don't have payroll taxes every month," I said.

"You do, but you only pay them every three months."

"You kill me."

"I'm waving a red flag at you," he said. You know what a red flag is, right? It's a warning."

I signed his check and handed it to him. "You're the best, Don, thank you."

He gave me a fatherly pat on the back.

* * *

Mike showed up, and I gave him three hundred dollars.

"That's enough to rent an apartment. You already got a wardrobe from your lady friend," I said.

It was true. When he came to the shop, he was dressed in clothes I knew they had not given him at DVI.

I told him how it was. I would be stretching to take him on. If I did, he had to do the work and learn what Elena, Gil, and I did.

"If you don't want to hook up, I'll help you out until you get a job you want to do. No pressure."

"I want in," he said.

"Not in," Elena said. "The shop belongs to George. No partners."

Mike grinned at Elena. "I get it. George is the chief cook and bottle-washer. Even at DVI he was in charge. I understand." He looked Elena up and down, scooted close to her, and the timbre of his voice changed. "Are you going with anyone?"

"Hands off," I answered for her, "unless she says different," I said.

"You walk through the door and want to fuck the boss's girl," Elena said. "Not copacetic."

"I'm getting on the wrong path here, Elena. Sorry, I came on to you. You're just so hot. I'm grateful for the help and for the job offer. If you'll have me, I'll do the best I can at whatever I'm assigned to do. I never tried to sell anything before, but I think I can learn."

Elena softened a little toward him. I don't know if he could tell, but I could.

Mike wanted white uniforms with his name like Gil wore. He wore half-boots spit-shined like in the Navy where he had started. Mike had been a sailor longer than me, and it had made him navy-organized, navy-clean, and navy-groomed.

A week in, Elena said how fast Mike was catching on.

"He totally overdoes it with the women, young or old. He goes on and on, and when I look over, his customer is smiling away."

Mike and Gil were getting better at figuring estimates. Like Ramirez, I charged five dollars for estimates with a promise to give it back to the client in cash if we got the job. Ramirez had the right idea. Insurance estimates can be time-consuming. It means looking up pricing and figuring out hours to repair a project, depending on the size of the job.

"Reminds me of you when you started. By the time the guy customer signs his car over to you, he's halfway in love. And you manage to keep the women from hating you too."

* * *

I asked Elena to get me the chief adjuster, Henry Bell, at Farmer's Auto Claims.

She said, "I tried to reach him to ask him about the new program where they immediately write a check for the approved estimate of repairs and give it to either the shop or the customer, payable to both parties. He didn't call me back."

Elena gave me the number. I went upstairs and called him.

He answered on the first ring.

I told him who I was. We chatted a little bit. He asked right away about Elena. Elena had shown him around the shop when he had come over to check us out. A man has to love it when a woman like Elena gives you her undivided attention.

"I am extremely grateful for your trust and confidence, as evidenced by the work you continue to send us, but Henry, I have a problem."

"Tell me the problem."

"I can't afford to wait for payment like I'm doing. I have one car in the shop from you being worked on, so I can't count that one. I have a total of ten thousand one hundred dollars that we've billed Farmers that I am waiting to be paid on. I would not bug you like this if I didn't need the money."

"Tell you what, Champ. When I hang up the phone, I'll go visit accounts payable, and I will get you paid sure enough right away."

What I was hearing was like a miracle.

"That would be fantastic," I said.

I went to tell Elena.

"What a solid. Be nice if Intrastate would do it. They owe you twice that much."

"I'll give it a shot, but I'm taking a breather for a day. I really didn't want to call him about needing money."

"It's your money. You earned it," she said. "You not asking for a loan."

Mike was with Gil and a customer. The rush had subsided.

"Winchell's time!" I declared as happy as could be.

"I was thinking of a quickie." Elena was catching up to me as I headed for my car.

"I need something sweet," I said.

"You beast!" She punched my shoulder.

"Ouch!"

Winchell's was a donut shop we frequented. We had coffee at the shop, but we still got it at Winchell's when we went there for our sugar fix.

Chapter 19
Elena Kind of Moves In

Elena was bent over the desk, her fingers gripping the edge tightly. I was behind her, my body pressed against hers, feeling the warmth of her skin through the thin fabric of her blouse. Her legs were spread and braced, her breath coming in short, ragged gasps. My hands roamed over her breasts, feeling the soft, yielding flesh beneath my fingers. She moaned softly, the sound vibrating through the room.

Just then, the door swung open without warning. Mike, the only person in the entire place who never knocked, strolled in with a huge grin stretched across his face.

"Sorry, sorry," he said, though his tone suggested he was anything but.

I turned around, my face flushed with a mix of irritation and embarrassment. Elena didn't move, her body still trembling from the intensity of the moment.

"You are such an asshole, Mike. Fuck off!" Elena was pissed.

We got dressed in silence, exchanging looks that spoke volumes but saying nothing. Just as we were about to discuss the intrusion, Gil's voice crackled over the intercom, breaking the charged silence.

"Henry at Farmers on the line. He said, George or Elena."

I was two feet from my desk. I picked up the phone.

"Henry, hi."

"If you want to run over in the morning after ten, I'll have all your checks ready for you. It's a little more than the number you gave me earlier."

"Damn, I owe you big time, Henry."

"Keep making us look good by turning out good work and making the customer happy. Do that, and all of us at Farmers are happy. For the car you have in the shop now, I'm giving you a check payable to Eastland Auto Center and our insured. When you deliver the car, and the customer is satisfied, have it endorsed, and you don't need to do any more billing to us."

"Henry, you are a trooper. I owe you."

Elena was looking at me and trying to listen, though it wasn't really possible to hear. I hung up.

"What was that all about?"

I told her.

We whooped and hollered like we'd won the New York Lottery, holding each other and bouncing around the office so that it was a wonder it didn't come crashing down with us in it. It was four in the afternoon, not long before closing time.

"Should we go back to Winchell's?" I said with a silly laugh.

"No more Winchells today."

Elena picked up the phone at my desk. There were two options for calling the shop floor: the public address system, which everyone heard, or the intercom, which Gil or Mike would answer if they were near a phone.

Elena called and announced over the intercom, "Mike, we're going to finish what you interrupted, so don't come upstairs. Got it?"

She hung up.

We laughed and fisted, and this time, I got her positioned on the sofa sideways. That night at my apartment was the first time Elena didn't go home at all.

* * *

In the morning, we got up early. She jogged with me and was out of breath halfway up the monster hill I took every morning. She stopped dead, bent over, gasping that she couldn't do another second of the craziness. The funny part was the way she clutched the adjustable sweat shorts that were mine so they wouldn't fall off while she was running. The oversized t-shirt of mine looked great on her, maybe better than it usually would have since it was sweaty enough from the run that it stuck to her torso in a very interesting fashion.

"Go," she said, waving me up the hill as she headed down. "Finish. I'm all jogged out. I'll walk back to the apartment."

I trudged on. When I was back, she was in the extra bedroom shower. I got in the master bedroom shower, and before we got dressed, we did some hugging and cuddling.

"You can't imagine how good I feel to have you here with me.

"I feel good about it, too," she said.

We kissed.

I could smell coffee. I never made coffee, but I had coffee and a coffee maker. The smell reminded me of how Sophia would make the coffee, fix breakfast, and then rush to get ready for work. I'd leave. She'd leave a half-hour after I did. I didn't regret the past, but I wondered why it didn't work. Maybe the problem was her grandparents always being around. I don't know. Maybe it was just me not wanting to really surrender to a married life.

* * *

It was the first time I rode in the passenger seat of my car. Elena drove us to work.

"Could be I have to fuck Henry to get more work," Elena said.

"You're joking," I said.

She was driving, her eyes ahead, but turned to see my response.

"It's just a fuck. Let me go to Farmers and pick up the checks."

"I don't want you to fuck him," I heard myself say.

She turned her eyes back to the road as traffic moved in, started, and stopped. She smiled.

"You love me, G. You do." She chuckled.

* * *

When Elena was back from picking up the checks, I called my accountant, Donald, and told him about Farmers paying up. He seemed as pleased as Elena and I were. I drove over to the bank and deposited the checks and several deposits from the safe. I wanted to see Holmberg, but he had someone in his office. I knew he'd appreciate hearing that Farmers would now be paying us upon completion of the work instead of making us carry the paper.

The ten thousand seven hundred from Farmers still left about eighteen thousand owed me from insurance companies. I was beginning to struggle. Thanks to the car painting we did, we were afloat. Painting cars in Los Angeles was like the jukebox in Juarez. Every day, we took on new jobs, just as the jukebox was constantly playing nickel tunes, sixty cents in Mexican currency.

Now, decades later, I believe the smart move would have

been to put in another paint booth and oven. I had the room and clients for it, and I had the ambition to paint more cars. Even if I didn't, the cost of painting a car then was less than ten dollars. Insurance work meant big ticket items that overshadowed the whole painting economy, with an average of about a thousand dollars per car.

* * *

Elena went home and was back right after I closed. She had with her a suitcase she had carried from her house. It wasn't that far, but still, it was a big suitcase.

"I'm not officially moving in," she said. "I do want to spend more quality time with you. I need clothes, and I'm going to learn how to jog like you."

Mike picked up the suitcase. I threw him the keys to put it in the trunk of my car.

Elena said, "Hug me, G."

* * *

Mike never rented the apartment I had given him the money for. Vicki, the girl he met on the bus, was a waitress at a waffle shop in downtown Los Angeles and made over fifty dollars a day in tips.[1] That was a bunch in those days, a week's pay for a person making minimum wage. He was living with her and didn't plan on going anywhere.

* * *

I don't think Elena fucked Henry, the chief adjuster, but after

---

1. Adjusted for inflation, $50.00 in 1962 is equal to $428.29 in 2020.

she met with him at his office to pick up the checks, there was an increase in the business we got. It wasn't substantial enough to compensate for the volume we were getting from Intrastate.

Donald had come in for his monthly accounting, and in the middle of the day, Elena and I brought in a platter of meat market tacos that the three of us chowed down on.

"I'm lucky this place isn't next door to me," Don said. "If it was, I'd be three hundred pounds, at least."

Elena said, "How do the books look?"

"I'm hoping you can convince the others to pay you like Farmers is doing now. What a blessing that would be."

Elena looked at me over her taco.

I knew what she was thinking.

"Intrastate who owes us big time does not pay that way. I talked to them already," I said.

"That's too bad. Consider cutting down the volume from them or pausing taking any business from them."

"Donald, no such thing. If I try that, we'll get cut off. I can't do that."

Donald shrugged. "You're the boss." Chewing on a taco. "Sooner or later, you have to do something if there isn't a slow-down from them."

* * *

Elena, fresh from the shower, was bent over her open suitcase on the bed, rummaging through it. The clothes she'd worn to work were in our joint laundry basket. From the clean laundry, I tossed her an oversized t-shirt she'd slept in before. She managed to slip it on without losing the towel wrapped around her wet hair, then snapped her suitcase closed.

"You can use the closet," I said. "It doesn't bite."

Both bedrooms had two closets each, all filled with my

clothes. Elena hung out with me as I moved clothes around to make room for her stuff.

"Okay," I said, pointing out the gap I'd made in the closet. "This space is all yours. If you run out of room, I'll start pruning. I have way too much. I don't use half of what I have."

"Are you sure?"

"I'm positive."

I pulled the towel off her hair and tossed it behind me.

She laughed at me or my aim. I looked over my shoulder and saw the towel had snagged the top of the hall door.

"You told me the story about your nighttime shop and stash caper. I never imagined you took this much."

"The locker thing," I corrected. "This might be one-tenth of what we kept. I took care of Alicia and Clara. They sold some of it."

"Wow, how exciting is that?"

"It wasn't exciting. It was crazy! I would never do it again, never."

Elena sighed with a nod. "You could have gone back to prison."

"Right. Not crazy. It was stupid. I didn't do it because I wanted all these clothes. I just did it."

"G, here's a subject change. Tell me the truth. Were you getting it on with both Alicia and Clara?"

I shrugged. "Clara had a boyfriend, now her current husband."

"Come on, G, tell me. I tell you everything."

"You never bring up your sex partners before me," I said. "And it's okay you don't."

"I'll tell you if you want. You tell me about that chick who kissed you at the shop like she was filming a love story."

"What do you want to know?"

"Did you fuck them both?"

"You mean separately?"

"What else would I mean?"

"I fucked them both, and we did threesomes from time to time."

Elena yelled like she had discovered gold in the backyard. "You scoundrel. I never did anything close," she said, laughing.

Now, I find myself pondering why I couldn't savor moments with Sophia as I did with Elena back then. Can one speak to their spouse in the same unrestrained manner as they do with a lover? Is the dialogue more passionate and unrestricted with a girlfriend? Yes, it is. Is conversation filtered with a spouse? Or could it be that Sophia and I were akin to mismatched puzzle pieces, while Elena and I seemed to align effortlessly?

Once we went to bed, Elena wanted details.

"Alicia and Clara were on the bed with me," I said.

"And then what?"

"It was my first time doing that," I confessed. "It just happened."

"Live wires," she said.

"Yeah, we were all live wires."

"What haven't you done?"

I rolled on top of her. "I haven't made love to you today."

Elena touched my lips with her index finger and said, "Repeat after me: Elena, I want to fuck you."

I chuckled. "I want to fuck you, Elena. Right now."

"Mm," she said, shivering visibly. "The word fuck is a turn-on for me."

* * *

When I unlocked the Brooklyn Avenue gate to the shop, a line formed in the parking lot. Everyone got in place to start the ball rolling. Gil and Mike were shadowing Elena and me, and we were doing a good job getting the clients set up for the day. The phone was ringing off the hook, and Emily, who had no cars to mask yet, was answering it. She paged Elena to the line, and Elena came back to me a few moments later.

"Looks like you're on your own tonight," she said. "Tonight, I'll be celebrating Aunt Edna's birthday."

"I don't remember you mentioning your Aunt Edna," I said.

"Family by proxy," she said. "She's been working the mortuary phones since Alexander Graham Bell."

"Who is Alexander Graham Bell?" I asked, laughing.

"Dummy—he invented the phone," Elena laughed. "I'll miss you tonight, G."

"Hey, I know he invented the phone. I was just testing you."

Laughs.

* * *

I got home late. I never like drinking alone. I wanted a drink, but opened a beer, took one sip, and put it down. Beer didn't work for me anymore. I settled for a Coke. I opened the freezer, grabbed a chilled mug, and poured the carbonated sugar into it. The quiet made me anxious. I took a shower. I turned the TVs on in my bedroom and living room and walked around in my skivvies. I called my neighbors. They would probably be busy this time of night, and I figured the answering machine would come on. It didn't. Emma picked up.

"Long time," I said.

"Well, I'll be," she said.

"Elena is at her aunt's house for the night."

"Ava is busy, but I'm free for the rest of the night. Give me thirty minutes."

* * *

I opened the door, and we hugged before I shut it.

"I'm telling you in advance. No argument when I give you money," I said.

"No argument," she said. "I promise it will be worth it for you."

"It always is."

"Was," she said, laughing. "That Elena is sticky."

"Sticky is good," I said, dropping my towel and getting in bed.

"I'll give you sticky, G."

When I woke up, I knew Elena wasn't there. There was no smell of coffee, and I could just feel it. In her sleep, Emma had turned away from me, her pillow a riot of red curls. She had a sprinkle of pale freckles and very pale skin, barely distinguishable from the white sheets. She had broad shoulders, a narrow waist, and I noticed her ass was absolutely fine. It was difficult leaving her, but work was waiting. I showered and bagged my clothes with Elena's laundry. I bent down and kissed Emma. She stirred.

"If you weren't so pretty, I'd marry you," I said.

She giggled herself awake.

I put a fifty in her hand. "Thanks, friend," I said. "I feel great this morning."

"Hey, this is way too much money. Get serious."

I kissed her again.

"Don't sell yourself short," I said. "You're worth more than that."

As I started out of the bedroom, she sat up, yawning and stretching. The sheet fell down, revealing her bare breasts.

"Hey, G. It would be easy to fall in love with you."

I turned to face her.

"Don't you dare," I said, laughing.

* * *

I wasn't surprised to see Elena had opened the shop twenty minutes early. Gil was there but not Mike. I got out of my car, and she walked to meet me halfway. I stopped and watched her.

"You have the finest legs and ass, made for those jeans."

"Only my legs and ass?"

Standing in the parking lot, we hugged and kissed. Once we were in the shop, Elena handed me a hot cup of coffee.

"Were you lonely without me?"

"I called my neighbors, and one of them came over."

"You can't do without pussy one night," she said.

"It wasn't about pussy. It was company."

"Why didn't you call me?"

"It was midnight. I didn't know how long the party was going to last."

I loved it when Elena put her hands on my face, and that's what she did.

"G, I've been wondering how long it would be before you pulled your zipper down with another." She didn't sound vindictive or upset.

"I didn't have to tell you."

Mike arrived on time and went right to work.

Gil was with one customer. Mike took another. Elena and I each had customers. Thanks to location, visibility, word of mouth, and especially Elena's DJ friend Pepe, we were very busy. I regularly paid Pepe. He was a great source of business. His radio plugs brought in customers from outside our area.

Elena ordered lunch for us. At noon, we ate hot beef sandwiches on great big chunks of homemade bread still warm when it was delivered. I sat in my chair, and Elena pulled up a chair across the desk from me. I picked up a napkin and dabbed at the corner of her lips. Her tongue flicked after the trace of sauce.

"Are you going back to your wife?"

"Not a chance. Why you ask that?"

"Do you want me to go back to my aunt's or hang out there for more nights?"

I had half of the sandwich up to my mouth, ready to bite. I put it back on the plate and looked at her.

"Elena, the girls are friends. It's sex for money. You know that."

"I thought they stopped accepting money from you."

"Well, she took it this morning."

She put her sandwich down on the plate and looked at it instead of me. "You mean she spent the night?"

"Elena, come on."

She picked up the sandwich, bit it, and set it back down on the plate, still looking at the bread instead of me. "What bed did you use?"

"My bed."

"You could have fucked her in the other room. I'm not changing the sheets when we get home."

"I'm guessing Emma made the bed and put it all in the laundry bag."

"You got it all covered."

"Elena, don't be mad."

"You don't love me."

"I do love you."

* * *

Elena went home with me that night. Before we talked about dinner, we had sex on one of the living room chairs. She sat on me, and I went for thirty minutes.

"Emma drained you. Are you sure you're done?"

"You're so nasty," I said, laughing. "I could have finished in five minutes,"

"I'm kidding, G." She gave me a two-second kiss. "You were delicious. I don't know how you can go that long."

I checked the bed. Emma had made it with clean bedding and put the sheets and pillowcases in the laundry bag.

We changed into shorts, shirts, and tennis shoes and headed to the pizza parlor. I knew Olivia worked at Shakey's, but I figured it was always busy. Maybe she wouldn't see me. Maybe she wasn't working there anymore.

"Everything is good here," I told Elena when we took a seat. To hear each other, we had to sit shoulder-to-shoulder and practically yell in each other's ears. The music was deafening, and the conversation of a whole lot of customers was just as loud.

Some things are meant to be. There were more than ten waitresses, and Olivia got our table. She was so cool she deserved an Academy Award.

"George, nice to see you," she said.

Elena picked up on it. I don't know how. Maybe it was the intro.

"Olivia, hi, this is Elena. Elena, this is Olivia."

Smiles exchanged.

We ordered cokes and two medium pizzas.

"How long did you see her for?"

I was surprised, but I know how to handle surprises. I tell the truth.

"I'd say three months. She spent weekends with me because she works all week."

Elena nodded her head.

"Maybe I should ask you more about your life before me?" I asked, biting into the molten pizza. A long stretch of cheese drew to a thread like a noodle, and I sucked it into my mouth.

Elena said, "I did a count when I was twenty. I figured I'd been with eleven dudes. Want details?"

I took her hand. "Only if you want to tell me."

Chapter 20
I Don't Have A Jealous Bone In My Body

When I first opened, the only supplier that would give me credit was the paint company. They saw the investment in the spray booth and oven. I showed the owner a copy of my master lease to prove that it was my shop. For all of the other vendors who supplied us, it was cash on delivery. Eventually, I referred each supplier to Mr. Holmberg at my bank to verify that I was a customer in good standing. Ramirez disagreed. He'd said if you pay cash, you don't have to worry about paying the bill at the end of the month. I shined that on, but there is wisdom to what he said.

I did the deposits every day. Every day, I had to figure out how much of the cash I needed to hold back for shop incidentals and the cash part of payroll that was not included in the paycheck. If Luis earned a hundred dollars and fifty was paid to him in a paycheck, the other fifty was cash. I needed cash. In the early sixties, a shop like mine didn't have to mess with credit cards. It was cash or check.

Elena came into the office as I was finishing up the bank deposit for the next day.

"I always wondered what it would be like to have sex with a white guy, a muscle-bound guy like Mike," Elena said.

It had been a couple weeks after my admission to Elena that Emma stayed over. My mind jumped on Elena bringing up Mike. It's a good thing that the deposits paperwork was done because I sure wasn't going to be thinking of anything else for a while.

"Have you looked in the mirror? You're whiter than I am, and I'm white."

"You know what I mean," she said. "I'm Mexican. Not sure why I'm so white. Anyway, want to hear this, or are you busy?'

I stopped and looked across my desk. I snapped the book closed and dropped the papers in my top drawer while she sat on one of two chairs.

"I'm all ears," I said.

"Mike has ribs like the washboard my mom kept in the laundry room."

I caught on. This was Mike, my friend who she didn't like when I introduced them."I know. I did time with him. Those abs come from hundreds of sit-ups a day. Even in the county jail he did them. You want to tell me that you did it with him?"

"It was a quickie, not an all-nighter like you had with Emma."

It hit me. I felt an impact on my stomach and heart. I didn't show her how I felt. One of my best classes in junior high school had been drama. My teacher, Mrs. Mitchell, said I had the gift of acting. I don't know how true it was, but I played it cool like the jealousy wasn't there. I don't know if it was anger or jealousy or what, just that my gut was full of it, and I acted like it was nothing.

"If you did it, what can I say? It's your pussy, not mine."

She got up, walked to the desk, put her palms on it, and leaned over. "Oh, that is so lame," she said and walked out.

Did she do it to get back at me or simply because she wanted a white dick? But my dick is white.

Fucking, Mike. He's a pussy hound. I told him not to mess with her. She had to make a pass for him to bite. I did time with him. He would not cross me. Or would he?

* * *

It was almost closing time when I returned to the shop floor. Mike was delivering finished jobs to customers, and Gil was writing an insurance estimate. Elena was just finishing up with a customer who picked out the paint color she wanted and was dropping off her car and picking it up the following day. I hung around overlooking everything as a boss might do. For the moment, there was nothing for me to do.

Elena finished with the customer and drove the car to the paint department, where it would be one of the first cars to be worked on in the morning.

I watched her get out of the car. She walked towards me. She was normal. This was Elena, beautiful, collected, fun Elena. I wasn't picturing her with Mike. I wasn't.

"Am I going home with you?" she asked.

I almost said, 'Not if you don't want to.'

"Sure, why not?" I asked.

"Are you pissed?"

"I'm not pissed," I said. I was feeling something, but I don't know what it was.

* * *

We got in the car. I turned the ignition switch. Elena touched my hand.

"G, I'm not sorry I did it. Don't be mad at Mike. I asked him."

I ignored her hand, put the car in reverse, and started to back up. My gut was churning. I didn't say anything.

Her door opened. I braked.

"I can see you don't want to discuss it," she said.

She got out and shut the door. I could have gotten out of the car. I could have tried to stop her. She was walking across the parking lot, probably to her aunt's house.

I drove home. After a shower, I was back in my car and headed to Shakey's. I sat at a table and asked my waitress if Olivia was in.

"She's in section six, over there," she said.

I moved over to section six. I asked myself why I was there. I didn't have an answer to that. Olivia appeared.

"Where is the lovely lady you were with?"

I picked up the menu and didn't reply. What was I going to say? She told me she did it with this guy I know and walked to her aunts to keep from coming home with me. No, I wouldn't say that.

"Olivia, want to come over tonight?" I asked.

She had a little hesitation. "Only if I can shower first. I don't want to smell up your apartment with pizza and beer."

I was suddenly lifted.

"You can shower and use any shirt in my closet."

"I get off at ten," she said.

"I know."

I got up and put a ten on the table.

"Looking forward to seeing you," I said.

✶ ✶ ✶

Olivia left at two, and I was up at six. I went jogging like I had eight hours of sleep. I took that steep street, remembering Elena caving and going back home. I had started like that, but like everything, if you do something long enough, you get used to it, and it gets easier. It was pretty tough that morning, but I got through it.

When I jog, I leave and come in from the front entrance. As soon as I opened the door, the aroma of coffee told me that Elena was there. Only she had a key to the apartment.

"Coffee is ready, G."

Sweaty as I was, she came in my arms. We kissed.

I never got my coffee, at least not right away. She took my hand and led me to the second bedroom, where the bed only had a bottom sheet and a pillow, never slept in. It could be I did not see right, but the bed looked slept in.

"Why here?" I asked as I dropped my running shorts. My T-shirt was already on the floor.

She lay on the bed naked.

"The other bed smells like last night," she said.

"Elena, it's me. I'm crazy."

She raised her arms. "Come to me, Mr. Crazy. Fuck me, no confessions, no talking."

We both made it. It was fantastic. We hit the shower and showered together, a first. We saw the time and rushed out. Elena's hair was towel dry. Our coffee was in a small thermos that we drank from on the way. We were the only ones with keys to the shop.

* * *

After so many years, the best recollections I have are when I didn't drink. I didn't drink with Olivia. Because my brain was not fogged with alcohol that night, that morning, my mind was clear.

At lunch, I asked Elena how she'd gotten there while I was jogging.

"I took a taxi last night."

I stopped eating and looked at her.

"Last night?"

"Roger that," she said, biting her hamburger and putting it down on the paper plate.

Olivia had spent the night with me. "You were there?"

"Roger that."

"Oh, Elena."

"That girl from the pizza joint screams like me."

"Oh, Elena."

The bed in the second bedroom *had* looked slept in.

"Did you get any sleep?" I asked.

"I did. I was thinking about getting in your bed after she left, but I fell asleep."

I put my hamburger down on my plate that was next to hers. I reached for her with both arms. She leaned over, and I held her cheeks with my hands, much like she often did to me.

"What are you waiting for? Kiss me," she said with a smile, a drop of mustard on her lip.

I wanted to say I love you. We kissed. We sighed. We went back to eating.

* * *

Mike cornered me that afternoon.

"She told you, huh?"

"Told me what?" I played dumb.

He grinned at me. "She told you, I know."

"Told me what?"

"Brother, you can fuck Vicki. I swear, it's okay."

"Thanks for the offer," I said.

"Serious, brother." He grinned. Oh, that grin. He put his hand out for a handshake.

I don't remember being truly pissed at Mike. I did wonder how Elena asked him.

Mike, want to fuck me? Hey Mike, want a quickie with me?

I still didn't know where and when. I never asked.

* * *

That night, Elena was with me at the apartment. We had some CC Waters. We fell out laughing, changing my linens together. I told Elena Mike's offer of doing Vicki to get even.

"G, she's not your type."

"My type or not, I wouldn't fuck her, period."

"I don't want to bring it up, but you should know it was quick. And I made him use a Trojan." I remembered Patty and me with the Trojans back when they were just for pregnancy protection.

I laughed.

"What?"

"You put a Trojan on him?"

"I didn't put it on him. I handed it to him and told him if he wanted in, he had to put it on. I could tell he'd never used one."

I could have been angry, but how could I be when Elena had come into my apartment while I was fucking Olivia and said nothing, hung out, and made coffee for us in the morning? Fuck, Elena was a trooper, possibly a one-of-a-kind.

"It's okay," she kept saying. "Now that I know how you look when you fuck from a distance, I'm okay with it." The liquor's anesthetic effect had a little to do with how cool we were about it all.

* * *

"I feel horrible that I didn't let you know I was here," she said. "I could have kept quiet that I stayed in the other bedroom. G, I think that girl digs you more than you think."

I kissed her until she stopped talking. I kissed her entire body. She moaned and twisted with pleasure, and I, thanks to Christine's teachings, felt good that I made her feel that good.

* * *

I've always insisted I do not have a jealous bone in my body, but I've had close calls. In the Elena era, I was married with a baby girl. My wife and I had agreed a divorce was imminent. We kept putting it off. The upcoming divorce wasn't Sophia's fault. It was mine. I didn't want to be tied down. I wanted freedom. I wanted a wife and babies, but I wanted to be free to do as I pleased. Imagine how unorthodox that is. I'm guilty as a sin. It would be easier to write this another way, but I'm not going in that direction.

About the Author

George Hatcher, formerly a consultant for high-profile wrongful death cases and a successful entrepreneur, has transitioned away from those roles to focus wholeheartedly on his writing. While he no longer consults for lawyers or oversees businesses, George is deeply committed to his literary craft. The COVID-19 pandemic has limited his extensive travels, prompting him to channel his energies into his writing. He now finds solace in Rancho Mirage, California, where he enjoys the company of his wife, Molly, three cats, and two macaws, all while passionately pursuing his latest writing projects.

A longer bio is on his website at http://georgehatcher.com/bio/bio.html

www.ingramcontent.com/pod-product-compliance
Lightning Source LLC
Chambersburg PA
CBHW050526100526
44581CB00008B/148/J